Step-by-Step Wedding Hairstyles
35 Easy Bridal Looks in 15 Minutes or Less

Author: Bella Darby

Brought to you by MyBrideHairs.com

Legal and Copyright Disclaimer

Copyright © 2026 Bella Darby. All rights reserved.

This book is published by Bella Darby & brought to you by mybridehairs.com.

No part of this publication may be reproduced, distributed, stored in a retrieval system, or transmitted in any form or by any means, including electronic, mechanical, photocopying, recording, or otherwise, without prior written permission from the copyright owner, except for brief quotations used in reviews or as permitted by applicable copyright law.

The information in this book is provided for general informational and educational purposes only. All hairstyle ideas, styling methods, preparation tips, and product suggestions are intended as general guidance. Results may vary depending on hair type, hair texture, hair condition, skill level, products used, tools used, and environmental conditions.

Readers should use their own judgment and care when trying any hairstyle, accessory, heated styling tool, or beauty product described in this book, and should always follow the manufacturer's instructions.

The author and publisher are not responsible for any injury, loss, damage, allergic reaction, or styling outcome resulting from the use or misuse of the information in this book.

This book is not intended to replace the advice or services of a licensed hairstylist, beauty professional, dermatologist, or other qualified professional.

Any third-party product, service, or website mentioned in this book is referenced for informational purposes only and does not imply endorsement.

For permissions, updates, and more bridal hair resources, visit:

MyBrideHairs.com

Get Your Free Bridal Hair Planner Kit

Thank you for reading **Step-by-Step Wedding Hairstyles.**

To help you **choose**, **practice**, and **perfect** your bridal look, I created a FREE Bridal Hair Planner Kit for readers of this book.

Inside your free bonus, you'll get:

- Bridal Hairstyle Trial Checklist
- Wedding Morning Hair Prep Checklist
- Quick Style Finder Sheet
- Bridal Hair Emergency Kit Checklist
- Hairstyle Practice Tracker

This bonus is designed to help you feel more prepared, more confident, and less stressed before your big day.

Download your free bonus here:

MyBrideHairs.com/bridal-kit

Table of Contents

Half-Up Hairstyles

16. Classic Half-Up Twist
17. Half-Up Braided Crown
18. Half-Up Bouffant
19. Curled Half-Up with Face-Framing Pieces
20. Half-Up Knot Style

Short Hair Bridal Styles

21. Soft Curled Bob
22. Twisted Side Pin Bridal Style
23. Crown Twist for Short Hair
24. Sleek Pinned Bob
25. Side-Swept Short Glam Waves

Quick Bridesmaid and Guest Styles

26. Quick Low Ponytail Twist
27. Side-Swept Ponytail Curls
28. Easy Textured Low Bun
29. Simple Braided Ponytail
30. Twisted Side Bun

Theme-Based Wedding Hairstyles

31. Boho Floral Braid
32. Beachy Bridal Waves
33. Vintage Hollywood Waves
34. Glam High Bun
35. Rustic Loose Side Braid

Accessories That Work
Hairstyles by Face Shape
Quick Fixes and Troubleshooting
Wedding Morning Game Plan

How to Use This Book

Planning your wedding hairstyle can feel exciting, but it can also feel overwhelming with so many choices available. This book was created to make that process easier by giving you a collection of beautiful, wearable wedding hairstyles that are simple to understand and easy to practice.

Inside, you will discover 35 elegant step-by-step wedding hairstyles, each designed to help you create a graceful bridal look in 15 minutes or less. From timeless updos to soft romantic styles, these hairstyles are meant to suit a wide range of hair lengths, textures, and wedding themes.

For the best experience, begin with the early chapters on hair preparation, essential tools, and basic styling techniques. These sections will give you the foundation you need before trying the hairstyles themselves. A little preparation can make a big difference in how well a style holds, how easy it feels to create, and how polished the final result looks.

When exploring the hairstyle chapters, choose a few styles that match your hair length, hair texture, comfort level, wedding theme, and desired overall look.

Rather than trying every style, choose your top favorites and do a few practices runs before the wedding day. This will help you discover which hairstyle feels most natural, flattering, and practical for your schedule and setting.

You can use this book in whatever way works best for you. You may read it from beginning to end, jump directly to the hairstyle tutorials, revisit the troubleshooting tips when needed, or use the sections on accessories, themes, and face shapes to refine your final choice.

Most importantly, remember that your wedding hairstyle does not need to be overly complicated to be beautiful. The best style is one that feels true to you, complements your overall bridal look, and allows you to enjoy your day with confidence.

Use this book as your guide, practice with patience, and trust the process. With the right style and a little preparation, you can create a wedding hairstyle that feels both elegant and personal.

Beautiful bridal hair starts with clarity, confidence, and a little practice.

Quick Style Finder

Choose your hairstyle based on these five things:

Hair length: short, medium, or long

Hair type: straight, wavy, curly, fine, or thick

Skill level: beginner, intermediate, or advanced

Wedding vibe: classic, romantic, boho, glam, beach, or rustic

Practical needs: veil, weather, time, and comfort

Pick three styles, practice them, photograph them, and choose the one that feels best and lasts the longest.

Best for Beginners

- Simple Chignon
- Soft Twisted Low Updo
- Loose Romantic Curls
- Classic Half-Up Twist
- Twisted Side Pin Bridal Style
- Quick Low Ponytail Twist
- Rustic Loose Side Braid

Best for Romantic Looks

- Soft Twisted Low Updo
- Loose Romantic Curls
- Floral Half-Up Waves
- Romantic Braided Bun
- Waterfall Braid with Curls
- Curled Half-Up with Face-Framing

Best for Classic Looks

- Simple Chignon
- Elegant French Twist
- Sleek Low Bun
- Knotted Bridal Bun

- Vintage Hollywood Waves

Best for Boho Looks

- Floral Half-Up Waves
- Braided Crown
- Side Braid Bridal Style
- Fishtail Bridal Braid
- Boho Floral Braid
- Rustic Loose Side Braid

Best for Glam Looks

- Side-Swept Curls
- Pinned-Back Hollywood Waves
- Side-Swept Short Glam Waves
- Vintage Hollywood Waves
- Glam High Bun

Best for Short Hair

- Soft Curled Bob
- Twisted Side Pin Bridal Style
- Crown Twist for Short Hair
- Sleek Pinned Bob
- Side-Swept Short Glam Waves

Best for Medium-Length Hair

- Simple Chignon
- Elegant French Twist
- Loose Romantic Curls
- Classic Half-Up Twist
- Easy Textured Low Bun

Best for Long Hair

- Simple Chignon
- Knotted Bridal Bun
- Romantic Braided Bun
- Braided Low Bun
- Half-Up Braided Crown
- Glam High Bun

Best for Veils

- Simple Chignon
- Elegant French Twist
- Sleek Low Bun
- Loose Romantic Curls
- Floral Half-Up Waves
- Romantic Braided Bun
- Pinned-Back Hollywood Waves

Best for Outdoor or Humid Weather

- Elegant French Twist
- Sleek Low Bun
- Knotted Bridal Bun
- Braided Low Bun
- Easy Textured Low Bun
- Glam High Bun

Best for Bridesmaids and Wedding Guests

- Side Braid Bridal Style
- Classic Half-Up Twist
- Soft Curled Bob
- Quick Low Ponytail Twist
- Side-Swept Ponytail Curls
- Simple Braided Ponytail
- Twisted Side Bun

Pick three styles, practice them, photograph them, and choose the one that feels best, looks best in photos, and lasts the longest.

Top 10 Easiest Hairstyles for Beginners

If you are new to hairstyling, start with styles that feel simple, forgiving, and easy to practice. You do not need advanced skills to create a beautiful bridal look. Many elegant wedding hairstyles are built from just a few beginner-friendly techniques, such as twisting, pinning, curling, and gathering the hair neatly.

This section highlights 10 of the easiest hairstyles in this book for first-time styling. These looks are quick to practice, easy to manage, and beautiful enough for weddings, bridal events, and special occasions.

Beginner tip: Start with **2 or 3 styles only**, practice them more than once, take photos in natural light, and choose the one that feels the most comfortable and flattering.

Simple styles often create the most effortless beauty.

1. Simple Low Bun

A timeless hairstyle that looks elegant without being difficult to create.

Best for: medium to long hair

Why it is easy: a simple twist-and-pin shape that is easy to control

Good choice if you want: a classic, neat bridal style

Beginner tip: leave a few soft strands near the face for a romantic finish

2. Half-Up Half-Down Twist

A soft and flattering style that keeps hair away from the face while still showing the length.

Best for: medium to long hair

Why it is easy: only the top sections need styling, so it feels less overwhelming

Good choice if you want: a soft and feminine look

Beginner tip: curl the loose hair first to add volume and movement

3. Side-Swept Curls

A glamorous hairstyle made by curling the hair and gently securing it to one side.

Best for: medium to long hair

Why it is easy: the method is simple, curl, sweep, and pin

Good choice if you want: a romantic or evening bridal look

Beginner tip: let the curls cool fully before brushing or touching them

4. Soft Loose Waves

A relaxed and graceful hairstyle that does not need perfect structure to look beautiful.

Best for: short, medium, or long hair

Why it is easy: soft waves are forgiving and easy to adjust

Good choice if you want: a natural, effortless look

Beginner tip: use a light hairspray so the waves stay soft, not stiff

5. Sleek Low Ponytail

A modern and polished hairstyle that is simple to create and easy to wear.

Best for: medium to long hair

Why it is easy: it mainly involves smoothing, brushing, and securing

Good choice if you want: a clean, minimal bridal style

Beginner tip: wrap a small section of hair around the elastic for a more finished look

6. Messy Low Bun

A soft, relaxed bun that is one of the most forgiving styles for beginners.

Best for: medium to long hair

Why it is easy: small imperfections blend in naturally and still look pretty

Good choice if you want: a romantic or boho-inspired finish

Beginner tip: gently loosen the bun after pinning to create more volume

7. Simple Side Braid

A charming hairstyle that feels familiar because it is based on a basic braid.

Best for: medium to long hair

Why it is easy: many beginners already know the basic three-strand braid

Good choice if you want: a sweet, youthful, or relaxed bridal look

Beginner tip: keep the braid slightly loose for a softer and fuller result

8. Twisted Crown Front

A pretty style that creates a crown-like effect without needing a full braid.

Best for: short, medium, or long hair

Why it is easy: twisting is usually easier than braiding

Good choice if you want: an elegant front detail with minimal effort

Beginner tip: place a decorative pin where the twists meet for a bridal touch

9. Pinned-Back Front Sections

A quick and graceful look created by pinning back small front pieces of hair.

Best for: short, medium, or long hair

Why it is easy: it is fast, flexible, and easy to adjust

Good choice if you want: a simple style with a soft bridal feel

Beginner tip: add curls or waves to the rest of the hair for a prettier finish

10. Classic Chignon

A timeless bridal hairstyle that can still be beginner-friendly when kept low and simple.

Best for: medium to long hair

Why it is easy: low placement makes the shape easier to pin and control

Good choice if you want: a polished and traditional bridal look

Beginner tip: practice this style two or three times before the big day

How to Choose Your First Style

If you are not sure where to begin, start with the hairstyle that feels the easiest and most natural for you.

A great first choice is:

Simple Low Bun for classic elegance

Half-Up Half-Down Twist for softness and romance

Soft Loose Waves for a natural, effortless look

Sleek Low Ponytail for a modern finish

Messy Low Bun for a forgiving and beginner-friendly style

Try one or two styles first, take clear photos from the front, side, and back, and choose the one that makes you feel the most confident.

The best beginner hairstyle is the one that feels beautiful, comfortable, and easy to wear.

Best Hairstyles by Bridal Need

Every bride has different needs. Some want a timeless and elegant look, while others need a hairstyle that works with short hair, natural curls, humid weather, a veil, or a busy wedding schedule. The best bridal hairstyle is not just about beauty. It should also suit your hair type, comfort level, dress style, accessories, and wedding setting.

This section will help you choose the right hairstyle based on what matters most to YOU.

Pick the need that fits you best, then start with the recommended styles from this book.

Classic Bridal Look

If you love timeless beauty, polished structure, and elegant details, classic hairstyles are a strong choice. These styles pair beautifully with traditional gowns, cathedral veils, pearl accessories, and formal wedding settings.

Best options from this book:

- Simple Chignon
- Elegant French Twist
- Sleek Low Bun
- Classic Half-Up Twist
- Pinned-Back Hollywood Waves

Best for:

- formal ceremonies
- traditional bridal looks
- elegant dresses
- clean and refined styling

Why it works:

Classic hairstyles never feel dated. They look graceful in photos and usually hold their shape well throughout the day.

Romantic Bridal Look

Romantic hairstyles are soft, feminine, and full of movement. They often include curls, twists, loose texture, braids, and face-framing pieces that create a gentle and dreamy finish.

Best options from this book:

- Loose Romantic Curls
- Side-Swept Curls
- Floral Half-Up Waves
- Romantic Braided Bun
- Curled Half-Up with Face-Framing Pieces

Best for:

- garden weddings
- soft bridal makeup
- lace dresses
- brides who want a delicate look

Why it works:
Romantic styles feel beautiful without looking too stiff or overdone.
Boho or Natural Bridal Look
Boho hairstyles feel relaxed, textured, and effortless. They are perfect for outdoor weddings, rustic venues, beach celebrations, and brides who want a softer, less structured style.

Best options from this book:

- Braided Crown
- Boho Floral Braid
- Beachy Bridal Waves
- Rustic Loose Side Braid
- Half-Up Braided Crown

Best for:

- beach weddings
- outdoor weddings

- rustic or boho themes
- floral accessories

Why it works:

Boho bridal hair looks best when it feels soft, natural, and slightly undone in the right way.

Glam Bridal Look

Glam bridal hairstyles are polished, confident, and photo-ready. These styles usually have more shine, shape, volume, or dramatic finish.

Best options from this book:

- Vintage Hollywood Waves
- Glam High Bun
- Side-Swept Short Glam Waves
- Sleek Low Bun
- Pinned-Back Hollywood Waves

Best for:

- evening weddings
- statement makeup
- fitted gowns
- modern glamorous styling

Why it works:

Glam styles create strong visual impact and look especially beautiful in wedding portraits.

Short Hair

Short hair can look every bit as bridal as long hair when styled with care and the right finishing touches. Pins, waves, side sweeps, and accessories can make short hair feel elegant and special.

Best options from this book:

- Soft Curled Bob
- Twisted Side Pin Bridal Style

- Crown Twist for Short Hair
- Sleek Pinned Bob
- Side-Swept Short Glam Waves

Best for:

- brides with bobs or shoulder-length cuts
- simpler styling routines
- lighter, more comfortable looks

Why it works:
Short hair often styles faster and can look very polished with less effort.

Medium-Length Hair
Medium-length hair is one of the most flexible lengths for bridal styling. It works well for buns, half-up styles, curls, and twists without feeling too heavy.

Best options from this book:

- Soft Twisted Low Updo
- Romantic Braided Bun
- Classic Half-Up Twist
- Curled Half-Up with Face-Framing Pieces
- Twisted Side Bun

Best for:

- versatile styling
- easy pinning
- balanced volume and movement

Why it works:
Medium-length hair is often easier to control and shape than very long or very short hair.

Long Hair
Long hair gives you many bridal options, from elegant buns to flowing curls and detailed braids. The main goal is to choose a style that feels secure and does not become too heavy as the day goes on.

Best options from this book:

- Simple Chignon
- Braided Low Bun
- Half-Up Braided Crown
- Side Braid Bridal Style
- Loose Romantic Curls

Best for:

- fuller looks
- detailed braids
- soft half-up styles
- statement bridal hair

Why it works:

Long hair gives you flexibility, fullness, and styling variety when supported properly.

Fine or Thin Hair

Fine hair looks best in styles that build gentle volume, lift, and texture without weighing the hair down too much.

Best options from this book:

- Half-Up Bouffant
- Side-Swept Curls
- Soft Curled Bob
- Floral Half-Up Waves
- Easy Textured Low Bun

Best for:

- brides who want more fullness
- soft shaping around the crown
- airy and romantic finishes

Why it works:

Fine hair benefits from teasing, texture spray, and lighter styles that create the look of more body.

Thick Hair

Thick hair holds many bridal styles beautifully, especially buns, twists, and braids. It may need more sectioning, stronger pins, and extra hold to stay polished.

Best options from this book:

- Knotted Bridal Bun
- Braided Crown
- Twisted Side Bun
- Glam High Bun
- Braided Low Bun

Best for:

- structured updos
- fuller styles
- stronger shape and support

Why it works:

Thick hair gives natural fullness, which can make bridal styles look rich and elegant.

Curly Hair

Curly hair already has movement, softness, and natural beauty. The goal is not to fight the curls, but to shape and support them in a way that feels bridal.

Best options from this book:

- Loose Romantic Curls
- Side-Swept Curls
- Curled Half-Up with Face-Framing Pieces
- Romantic Braided Bun
- Pinned-Back Hollywood Waves

Best for:

- natural texture
- soft volume
- romantic bridal looks

Why it works:
Curly hair adds built-in texture and softness, which can make bridal styles look fuller and more effortless.

Veil-Friendly Hairstyles

If you plan to wear a veil, choose a hairstyle that gives the veil a secure place to sit without flattening the whole look.

Best options from this book:

- Simple Chignon
- Sleek Low Bun
- Soft Twisted Low Updo
- Braided Low Bun
- Classic Half-Up Twist

Best for:

- brides wearing comb veils
- low veil placement
- longer ceremony styling

Why it works:

Low buns, low updos, and secure half-up styles usually give the best support for a veil.

Humid or Outdoor Wedding Weather

Humidity, wind, and heat can affect bridal hair quickly. Choose styles that hold shape well and do not depend too much on perfect smoothness.

Best options from this book:

- Sleek Low Bun
- Braided Low Bun
- Twisted Side Bun
- Easy Textured Low Bun
- Braided Crown

Best for:

- beach weddings
- garden weddings
- summer weddings

- long outdoor events

Why it works:
Secured updos and braids usually last better than loose styles in difficult weather.

Fastest and Easiest Styles
If you are short on time, new to hairstyling, or just want a less stressful option, begin with simple styles that are forgiving and easy to practice.

Best options from this book:

- Simple Chignon
- Classic Half-Up Twist
- Quick Low Ponytail Twist
- Easy Textured Low Bun
- Twisted Side Pin Bridal Style

Best for:

- beginners
- wedding week practice
- bridesmaids helping each other
- low-stress styling

Why it works:
Simple styles usually give the best results with the least pressure.

Best Styles for Bridesmaids or Wedding Guests

Not every style in this book has to be for the bride. Some are perfect for bridesmaids, sisters, mothers, or guests who want to look polished without taking too much time.

Best options from this book:

- Quick Low Ponytail Twist
- Side-Swept Ponytail Curls
- Easy Textured Low Bun
- Simple Braided Ponytail
- Twisted Side Bun

Best for:

- bridal party styling
- rehearsal dinner
- engagement events
- wedding guests

Why it works:

These styles feel elegant and event-ready without requiring too much time or complexity.

Final Tip

The best bridal hairstyle is not always the most detailed one. It is the one that feels comfortable, suits your hair, matches your wedding look, and helps you feel confident all day long.

Choose two or three styles that match your needs, practice them in advance, take photos, and trust the one that feels most like YOU.

Hair Preparation and Maintenance

A beautiful wedding hairstyle starts long before the first pin is placed. The way you care for your hair in the days and weeks before the wedding can affect how well your hairstyle looks, feels, and lasts. Hair that is too oily, too dry, or poorly prepared can make styling harder and reduce hold. **Good prep creates better results.**

Know Your Hair Type

Before choosing products or styles, understand your hair type and condition.

- **Straight hair:** smooth and elegant, but may need texture spray for better grip
- **Wavy hair:** flexible and easy to style, but may need anti-frizz support
- **Curly hair:** full of texture and volume, but needs moisture and gentle handling
- **Fine hair:** may need mousse or teasing for volume and hold
- **Thick hair:** often needs stronger pins, extra sectioning, and more control
- **Dry or damaged hair:** benefits from deep conditioning and less heat
- **Oily hair:** may need dry shampoo and lighter products near the roots

Choosing a style that works with your hair type will make the final result look better and last longer. **Work with your hair, not against it.**

Build Healthy Hair Before the Wedding

Healthy hair is easier to style and photograph beautifully. In the weeks before the wedding:

- trim split ends if needed
- use a deep conditioning mask once a week
- protect hair from too much heat
- drink enough water and eat well
- avoid major last-minute changes like new cuts, colors, or treatments

Small, steady care makes a big difference. **Healthy hair always styles better.**

What to Do Before the Wedding

30 Days Before

- choose 2 or 3 possible hairstyles
- start testing products and accessories
- trim or refresh hair if needed
- begin extra conditioning if hair feels dry

7 Days Before

- do a final trial of your chosen hairstyle
- wear it for a few hours to test hold and comfort
- check how it looks with accessories like veils, flowers, or clips

The Night Before

- wash your hair only if it suits your style and hair type
- avoid heavy oils or thick products
- prepare your tools, pins, sprays, and accessories in one place

Planning ahead helps avoid stress and surprises. **A calm plan leads to a better hairstyle.**

Wedding Morning Hair Prep

On the wedding day:

- begin with dry, detangled hair
- use only the products you need, such as mousse, texture spray, or smoothing serum
- section hair neatly before styling
- allow enough time so you do not have to rush

A clean, organized start makes styling much easier. **Good prep saves time and improves the final look.**

Final Thoughts

Wedding hair looks best when it is healthy, understood, and properly prepared. With the right care and planning, your chosen hairstyle will be easier to create, more comfortable to wear, and more likely to last throughout the celebration. **Preparation is the secret behind a beautiful bridal style.**

Tools You Actually Need

Creating a beautiful wedding hairstyle does **not** require a full salon kit. In most cases, you only need a few reliable tools to prep your hair, shape the style, secure it well, and help it last through the day. The right tools save time, reduce stress, and make styling much easier.

Must-Have Tools

Hairbrush

A good brush helps detangle hair and smooth it before styling. It also helps create a neat base for buns, ponytails, and twists.

Wide-Tooth Comb

This is especially helpful for curly, wavy, or fragile hair because it removes knots more gently.

Tail Comb

A tail comb is perfect for making neat parts, sectioning hair, and teasing the crown for extra volume.

Hair Elastics

Use soft, snag-free elastics to hold ponytails, buns, braids, and half-up styles securely.

Bobby Pins

Bobby pins are one of the most important bridal hair tools. They help secure buns, twists, and loose sections. Choose pins close to your hair color for a cleaner finish.

Sectioning Clips

These clips keep hair out of the way while you work, making the process more organized and easier.

Hairspray

A good hairspray helps the style stay in place and controls flyaways. Choose flexible hold for softer styles or stronger hold for long events and humid weather.

Mirror Setup

A main mirror and a hand mirror help you check the front, sides, and back of the hairstyle.

Heat Styling Tools

Hair Dryer

A dryer helps shape the hair, smooth roots, and prepare it for styling.

Curling Iron or Wand

Perfect for soft curls, waves, and romantic face-framing pieces.

Straightener

Useful for sleek buns, polished ponytails, and smoothing frizz.

Heat Protectant

Always use this before heat styling to reduce damage.

Helpful Styling Products

Texturizing Spray

Adds grip and body, especially for fine or freshly washed hair.

Mousse

Helps create volume and soft hold.

Smoothing Serum

Controls frizz and adds shine. Use only a small amount.

Dry Shampoo

Adds grip at the roots and helps absorb oil.

Finishing Accessories

Decorative Pins and Clips

Pearl pins, crystal clips, and floral pins can quickly make a simple hairstyle look more bridal.

Headbands, Hair Vines, and Flowers

These work well for romantic, boho, or garden-inspired looks.

Veil or Tiara

Always test these during a practice run so you know the hairstyle can support them properly.

Beginner Bridal Hair Kit

If you are new to styling, start with this simple kit:

- hairbrush
- wide-tooth comb
- tail comb
- hair elastics
- bobby pins
- sectioning clips
- hairspray
- texturizing spray
- curling iron or straightener
- hand mirror

You do not need every tool on the market. A small, dependable set is often enough to create beautiful wedding hairstyles with confidence.

Simple tools. Less stress. Better results.

Shop Our Recommended Bridal Hair Tools

To make your styling journey easier, we have listed our favorite beginner-friendly bridal hair tools and accessories on our website. These include brushes, combs, bobby pins, clips, curling tools, sprays, and decorative accessories.

Browse our recommended tools at MyBrideHairs.com/products

Basic Techniques

Before trying full wedding hairstyles, it helps to learn a few basic techniques first. These simple skills will make styling easier, faster, and less stressful. Once you understand the basics, you will feel more confident creating curls, braids, buns, and updos that look beautiful and stay in place.

Brushing and Sectioning

A smooth hairstyle starts with properly prepared hair. Brushing removes tangles and creates a clean base for styling. If your hair is straight or slightly wavy, use a paddle brush. If your hair is curly or textured, use a wide-tooth comb to avoid breakage. Start at the ends and work your way up slowly.

Sectioning makes styling much easier. Divide your hair into smaller parts using clips or soft ties. This helps you work neatly and keeps everything under control.

Quick tips

- Fully detangle before styling
- Use clips to separate sections
- Keep sections neat and even

Curling Techniques

Curls add softness, shape, and volume to many wedding hairstyles. You can use a curling iron, flat iron, rollers, or heatless methods depending on your hair type and the look you want. Always apply heat protectant before using hot tools.

Take small sections of hair, wrap them around the tool, hold for a few seconds, and release gently. Let curls cool before touching them so they last longer. Smaller sections usually hold better and give more control.

Quick tips

- Use heat protectant every time
- Curl away from the face for a soft bridal look
- Let curls cool before loosening them

Braiding Techniques

Braids add texture and detail to wedding hairstyles. They can look neat and elegant or soft and romantic. Start with a simple three-strand braid by dividing the hair into three equal parts and crossing each outer section over the middle.

Do not worry if the braid is not perfect at first. Slightly loose braids can still look beautiful, especially for a romantic bridal style.

Quick tips

- Start with even sections
- Keep your hands close to the head
- Gently loosen the braid for a fuller look

Updo Techniques

Updos are popular for weddings because they look elegant and stay secure. Most updos are created by twisting, folding, or wrapping the hair, then pinning it into place. Build the hairstyle step-by-step instead of trying to do everything at once.

Secure the base well first, then shape the rest of the style. Use bobby pins for hold and check the look from the front, side, and back as you go.

Quick tips

- Secure the base first
- Cross bobby pins for stronger hold
- Leave a few soft strands out for a romantic finish

Quick Fixes with Pins, Ties, and Sprays

Small tools can make a big difference. Bobby pins help secure loose pieces, hair ties create the base for many styles, and hair spray helps the finished look stay in place. Choose pins that match your hair color when possible.

Use spray lightly and from a short distance away to avoid making the hair stiff. A little product is often enough.

Quick tips

- Keep extra pins nearby
- Use small elastics for hidden support

- Spray lightly for a natural finish

Final Practice Advice

These basic techniques are the foundation of almost every hairstyle in this book. Practice them a few times before trying your full bridal look. The more comfortable you are with sectioning, curling, braiding, and pinning, the easier styling will feel.

Wedding hair does not need to be perfect to be beautiful. A soft, secure, and natural look often feels the most special.

Classic Bridal Updos

Classic bridal updos are timeless for a reason. They look **elegant, polished, and graceful** in almost any wedding setting. Whether you want a soft low bun, a neat chignon, or a refined French twist, a classic updo helps keep your hair secure while letting your face, veil, jewelery, and dress stand out beautifully.

These styles work especially well for brides who want a look that feels **clean, romantic, and sophisticated** without chasing short-term trends. They also tend to photograph well from different angles and can stay in place longer during the ceremony, photos, and reception with the right prep.

How to Choose the Right Classic Updo

- Choose a style based on your **hair length**. Low buns and chignons usually work best for medium to long hair, while shorter hair may need pins, padding, or a softer twisted style.
- Match the updo to your **dress neckline**. High necklines pair well with neat buns or twists, while off-shoulder or sweetheart necklines look lovely with softer, more romantic updos.
- Think about your **veil or accessories** first. Some updos hold veils, combs, and floral pins better than others.
- Pick a style that suits your **hair texture**. Fine hair may need volume support, while thick hair may need stronger sectioning and extra pins.
- Be honest about your **skill level**. Some updos are beginner-friendly, while others need more practice or a helper.
- Consider the **weather and venue**. Outdoor, humid, or windy weddings usually need more secure updos with stronger hold.
- Think about your **comfort**. A style that feels too tight or heavy may become annoying during a long wedding day.
- Choose a look that feels like **you**. A classic updo should enhance your natural beauty, not make you feel unlike yourself.

Tips for Beautiful Classic Updos

- Practice the style at least **2 to 3 times** before the wedding day.

- Work on **dry hair** unless the style specifically needs damp prep.
- Use **texture spray or dry shampoo** if your hair is too soft or slippery.
- Keep **bobby pins, clear elastics, and hair spray** ready before you begin.
- Curl or bend a few sections first if you want a softer, fuller updo.
- Leave a few face-framing strands out only if it suits your face shape and overall look.
- Secure the style in layers instead of trying to pin everything at once.
- Check the updo from the **front, sides, and back** in a mirror.
- Do a quick **movement test** by turning your head gently to make sure the style stays secure.
- Take a few phone photos in natural light to see how the style really looks on camera.
- Keep an **emergency mini kit** nearby with extra pins, a comb, and travel-size hair spray.
- Avoid trying a totally new product on the wedding day.

A classic updo should feel SECURE, FLATTERING, and TIMELESS. That is the goal.

1. Simple Chignon

Best for: Medium to long hair

    Hair type: Straight, wavy, lightly curly

    Skill level: Beginner

    Time needed: 10-15 minutes

    Best for: Ceremony, reception, classic weddings

    Works with: Veil, pearl pins, floral clips

    Hold level: Medium to strong

The chignon is one of the most timeless bridal hairstyles of all. Worn low at the back of the head, it creates a soft and graceful look that pairs beautifully with both traditional and modern wedding dresses. This hairstyle is especially loved by brides who want elegance without too much complexity.

    You'll Need

- Hairbrush or comb
- Hair elastic
- Bobby pins
- Hair spray
- Optional: curling iron, pearl pins, decorative comb

Before You Start

For best results, work with dry hair that has a little texture. If your hair is very soft or slippery, use a light texture spray or dry shampoo before styling. This helps the bun stay secure for longer.

Step-by-Step

Step 1: Brush your hair gently to remove tangles and smooth the surface.

Step 2: Gather your hair into a low ponytail at the nape of your neck and secure it with an elastic.

Step 3: Twist the ponytail loosely and wrap it around the base to form a bun.

Step 4: Secure the bun with bobby pins, placing them around the base and into the center where needed.

Step 5: Gently loosen a few small sections near the crown or around the face if you want a softer romantic finish.

Step 6: Set the style with hair spray and add decorative pins if desired.

SIMPLE CHIGNON
6-STEP GUIDE

STEP
1

Brush your hair gently to remove tangles and smooth the surface.

STEP
2

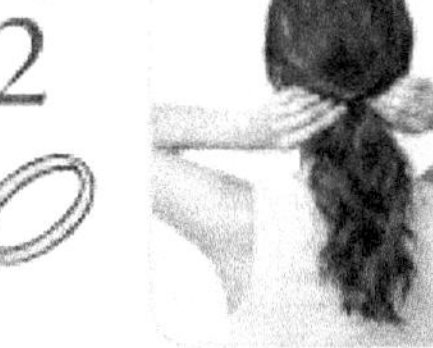

Gather your hair into a low ponytail at the nape of your neck and secure it with an elastic.

STEP
3

Twist the ponytail loosely and wrap it around the base to form a bun.

STEP
4

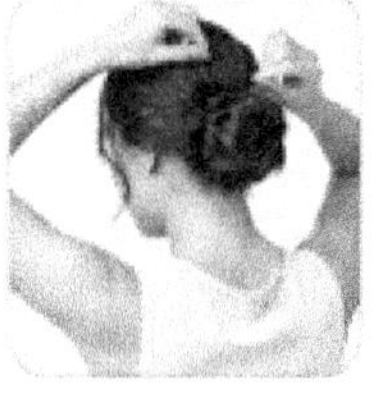

Secure the bun with bobby pins, placing them around the base and into the center where needed.

STEP
5

Gently loosen a few small sections near the crown or around the face if you want a softer romantic finish.

STEP
6

Set the style with hair spray and add decorative pins if desired.

Common Mistakes

- Bun feels loose after a few minutes
- Hair looks too flat at the crown
- Pins show too much
- Bun sits unevenly

Quick Fixes

- Cross two bobby pins over each other for stronger hold
- Lightly tease the crown before making the ponytail
- Tuck visible pins under the bun shape
- Check the bun from the back with a mirror before spraying

Make It Your Own

- Add pearl pins for a classic bridal finish
- Leave soft strands around the face for a romantic look
- Place the veil just above or below the bun depending on your preference

Heads-Up

This style is easy to do, but it looks even better after one or two practice runs. Brides with layered hair may need a few extra pins to keep shorter pieces in place.

The simple chignon is proof that elegance does not need to be complicated.

2. Elegant French Twist

Best for: Medium to long hair

Hair type: Straight, smooth, lightly wavy

Skill level: Intermediate

Time needed: 12-15 minutes

Best for: Formal weddings, evening receptions, classic bridal looks

Works with: Veil, jeweled comb, pearl accessories

Hold level: Strong

The French twist is a polished and refined hairstyle that gives a bride a graceful and sophisticated look. It has been a bridal favorite for decades because it instantly makes the hair appear neat, elevated, and elegant.

You'll Need

- Fine-tooth comb
- Bobby pins
- Hair spray
- Optional: smoothing serum, decorative comb

Before You Start

This style works best when the hair is smooth and easy to control. If needed, use a small amount of serum to tame frizz, but do not use too much or the hair may become slippery.

Step-by-Step

Step 1: Brush the hair back and gather it low at the back of your head as if making a low ponytail.

Step 2: Twist the gathered hair upward toward the crown.

Step 3: Fold the twist inward so the ends are tucked inside.

Step 4: Secure the twist with bobby pins along the seam.

Step 5: Gently smooth the outer layer with your hands or comb.

Step 6: Finish with hair spray and add a comb or bridal accessory if desired.

ELEGANT FRENCH TWIST
6-STEP GUIDE

STEP 1

Brush the hair back and gather it low at the back of your head as if making a low ponytail.

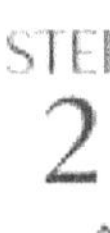 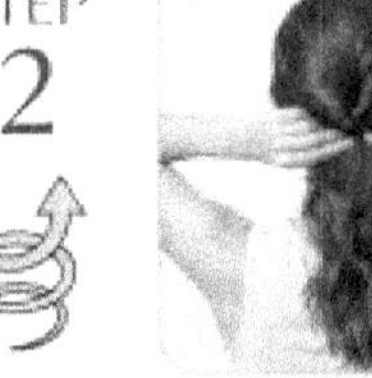

STEP 2

Twist the gathered hair upward toward the crown.

STEP 3

Fold the twist inward so the ends are tucked inside.

STEP 4

Secure the twist with bobby pins along the seam.

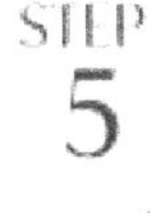  

STEP 5

Gently smooth the outer layer with your hands or comb.

STEP 6

Finish with hair spray and add a comb or bridal accessory if desired.

Common Mistakes

- Twist collapses in the center
- Ends poke out
- Hair feels too tight and stiff
- Style looks uneven from one side

Quick Fixes

- Pin along the full seam, not just the middle
- Tuck ends deeper before the final pins
- Pull slightly at the crown to soften if needed
- Check both side views in a mirror before final spray

Make It Your Own

- Add a jeweled comb on one side
- Leave a side part for a softer bridal feel
- Pair with statement earrings for a very elegant finish

Heads-Up

This hairstyle looks simple, but the balance and pin placement matter. Practice at least twice before using it on the wedding day.

The French twist is ideal for brides who want a clean, graceful, and truly timeless silhouette.

3. Sleek Low Bun

Best for: Medium to long hair

    Hair type: Straight, smooth, relaxed wavy

    Skill level: Beginner to intermediate

    Time needed: 10-12 minutes

    Best for: Minimalist weddings, modern brides, formal ceremonies

    Works with: Center part, veil, crystal comb, simple accessories

    Hold level: Strong

The sleek low bun is perfect for brides who love a modern, clean, and elegant style. It looks chic, polished, and sophisticated without feeling overly complicated. This hairstyle pairs especially well with structured dresses, satin fabrics, and minimal bridal styling.

    You'll Need

- Brush
- Tail comb
- Hair elastic
- Bobby pins
- Hair gel or smoothing cream
- Hair spray

Before You Start

This style looks best when the hairline and surface are neat. Use only a small amount of gel or smoothing cream to avoid making the hair look greasy.

Step-by-Step

Step 1: Create a center or side part, depending on the look you prefer.

Step 2: Brush the hair back smoothly into a low ponytail.

Step 3: Secure with an elastic at the nape of the neck.

Step 4: Twist the ponytail and wrap it neatly around the base.

Step 5: Pin the bun securely, keeping the shape tight and clean.

Step 6: Smooth flyaway and finish with hair spray.

SLEEK LOW BUN
6-STEP GUIDE

STEP 1

Create a center or side part, depending on the look you prefer.

STEP 2

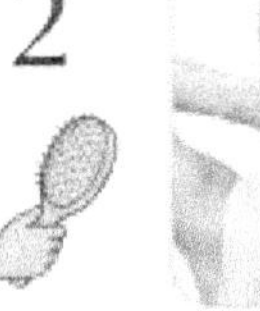

Brush the hair back smoothly into a low ponytail.

STEP 3

Secure with an elastic at the nape of the neck.

STEP 4

Twist the ponytail and wrap it neatly around the base.

STEP 5

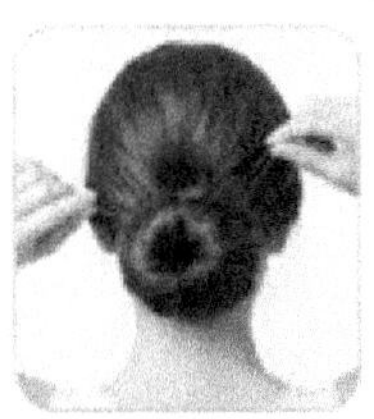
Pin the bun securely, keeping the shape tight and clean.

STEP 6

Smooth flyaways and finish with hair spray.

Common Mistakes

- Hair looks greasy instead of sleek
- Bun looks too small or flat
- Flyaway appear around the crown
- Parting line looks uneven

Quick Fixes

- Use less product and more spray if needed
- Loosen the bun slightly to create better shape
- Smooth the crown with a toothbrush or small brush
- Use a tail comb to sharpen the part

Make It Your Own

- Add a pearl veil comb above the bun
- Use a side part for a softer look
- Keep earrings bold and accessories minimal for a modern bridal feel

Heads-Up

This style is beautiful for brides who love a polished finish, but it can highlight uneven sectioning or visible pins if rushed.

A sleek low bun is simple, elegant, and effortlessly refined.

4. Soft Twisted Low Updo

Best for: Medium to long hair

    Hair type: Straight, wavy, curly

    Skill level: Beginner

    Time needed: 12-15 minutes

    Best for: Romantic weddings, garden weddings, soft bridal looks

    Works with: Flowers, pearl pins, soft veil placement

    Hold level: Medium

This hairstyle gives the beauty of a classic updo with a softer, more romantic touch. Instead of a tight bun or firm twist, the hair is gently twisted and pinned to create texture and softness.

    You'll Need

- Brush
- Hair elastic
- Bobby pins
- Curling iron, optional
- Hair spray

Before You Start

This style looks even prettier when the hair has a little wave or soft curl. If your hair is straight, lightly curling the ends first can add more texture and body.

Step-by-Step

Step 1: Brush through the hair and lightly curl the lengths if desired.

Step 2: Divide the hair into two or three sections.

Step 3: Twist one section at a time toward the back of the head.

Step 4: Pin each twisted section low at the back, layering them softly over one another.

Step 5: Adjust the shape to create a full but relaxed updo.

Step 6: Pull out a few face-framing strands if desired and finish with spray.

SOFT TWISTED LOW UPDO
6-STEP GUIDE

STEP 1
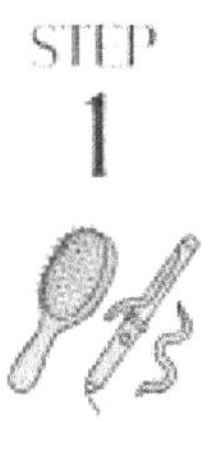

Step 1: Brush through the hair and lightly curl the lengths if desired.

STEP 2

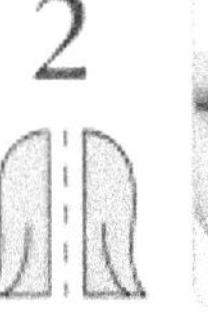

Step 2: Divide the hair into two or three sections.

STEP 3

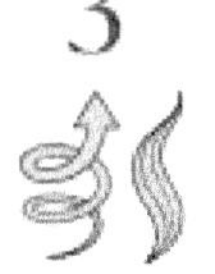

Step 3: Twist one section at a time toward the back of the head.

STEP 4

Step 4: Pin each twisted section low at the back, layering them softly over one another.

STEP 5

Step 5: Adjust the shape to create a full but relaxed updo.

STEP 6

Ste 6: Pull out a few face-framing strands if desired and finish with spray.

Common Mistakes

- Twists look messy instead of soft
- Pins do not hold the sections securely
- One side looks fuller than the other
- Style falls flat too quickly

Quick Fixes

- Twist sections evenly before pinning
- Use more pins underneath, not just on top
- Step back and compare both sides in a mirror
- Add a little teasing at the crown for extra fullness

Make It Your Own

- Add tiny flowers for a garden wedding
- Pair with soft curls around the face
- Use a side part for a more romantic feel

Heads-Up

This style is forgiving, which makes it beginner-friendly, but do not rush the shaping. Small adjustments make a big difference.

The soft twisted low updo is perfect for brides who want timeless beauty with a gentle romantic finish.

5. Knotted Bridal Bun

Best for: Medium to long hair

Hair type: Straight, wavy

Skill level: Intermediate

Time needed: 12-15 minutes

Best for: Classic weddings, modern weddings, elegant evening looks

Works with: Decorative combs, pearl accents, sleek veils

Hold level: Strong

The knotted bridal bun offers a refined look with a little extra detail. Instead of a standard wrapped bun, sections of the hair are twisted or folded into a knotted effect that adds texture while keeping the look polished.

You'll Need

- Comb
- Hair elastic
- Bobby pins

- Hair spray
- Optional: smoothing cream

Before You Start

This style works best when the hair is brushed smooth and divided cleanly. A little patience is important because the shape needs to look balanced.

Step-by-Step

Step 1: Gather your hair into a low ponytail.

Step 2: Divide the ponytail into two or three sections.

Step 3: Twist and loop each section around the base, creating a knotted shape.

Step 4: Pin each section carefully, hiding the ends underneath.

Step 5: Adjust the loops to create a full and elegant bun.

Step 6: Finish with hair spray and bridal accessories if desired.

KNOTTED BRIDAL BUN
6-STEP GUIDE

STEP 1

Gather your hair into a low ponytail.

STEP 2

Divide the ponytail into two or three sections.

STEP 3

Twist and loop each section around the base, creating a knotted shape.

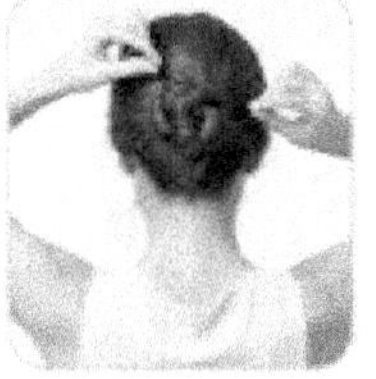

STEP 4

Pin each section carefully, hiding the ends underneath.

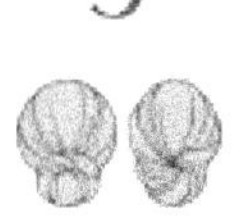

STEP 5

Adjust the loops to create a full and elegant bun.

STEP 6

Finish with hair spray and add a comb or bridal accessory if desired.

Common Mistakes

- Knot shape looks messy
- Ends stick out
- Bun shape becomes too tight and small
- Sections do not blend well

Quick Fixes

- Pin one section at a time before moving to the next
- Tuck ends under the bun before final pinning
- Gently loosen the loops for a fuller shape
- Smooth the surface lightly with your fingers

Make It Your Own

- Add a jeweled comb to one side
- Keep the crown sleek for a formal look
- Use soft strands near the face for a more romantic finish

Heads-Up

This style gives a beautiful result, but it needs a little more attention to detail than a basic bun. Practice helps the knot shape look intentional and elegant.

The knotted bridal bun blends timeless grace with a little extra design detail.

Romantic Soft Styles

Romantic soft hairstyles are perfect for brides who want a look that feels **elegant, gentle, and effortless**. These styles are designed to create a soft and flattering finish with loose curls, light twists, soft volume, and delicate details. They work beautifully for weddings that feel classic, garden-inspired, boho, intimate, or simply graceful.

One of the best things about romantic soft styles is that they do not look too stiff or overly formal. Instead, they create a natural and timeless beauty that feels warm, feminine, and easy to wear. Whether you choose a half-up look, soft curls, a braided detail, or a loose bun, these hairstyles can help you look polished while still feeling like yourself.

Romantic soft styles are also a great choice because they suit many hair lengths, face shapes, and wedding themes. With the right preparation, the right accessories, and a style that matches your hair type, you can create a bridal look that feels both beautiful and comfortable throughout the day.

How to Choose the Right Romantic Soft Style

- Choose a style that matches your **hair length**
    - Loose curls and half-up styles work well for medium to long hair
    - Soft pinned styles and side-swept looks can work well for shorter hair
- Think about your **hair type**
    - Fine hair may need added texture or light teasing for volume
    - Thick hair may hold soft curls and twists better
    - Curly or wavy hair can create a naturally romantic look with less effort
- Match the hairstyle to your **wedding theme**
    - Garden, outdoor, beach, and boho weddings pair beautifully with softer styles
    - Classic weddings can also look stunning with polished soft waves or elegant loose buns
- Consider your **dress neckline and details**

- ○ Off-shoulder and sweetheart necklines look beautiful with soft curls and half-up styles
  - ○ High necklines often pair better with softer updos or pinned-back looks
- Decide how much **hold and comfort** you need
  - ○ If you want movement and softness, choose looser styles
  - ○ If your wedding is outdoors or in humid weather, choose a romantic style with stronger pinning and hold
- Think about whether you want to wear a **veil or hair accessories**
  - ○ Loose buns and half-up styles often work well with veils
  - ○ Soft waves can be enhanced with floral pins, pearl clips, or delicate combs
- Be honest about your **skill level**
  - ○ Some soft styles are beginner-friendly
  - ○ Others may look easy but need practice to balance softness with hold

Tips for Getting the Best Results

- Start with **clean, fully dry hair** unless the style works better on second-day hair
- Use a **heat protectant** before curling or styling
- Add **texture spray or mousse** if your hair is too soft or slippery
- Do a **trial run** before the wedding day to see how the hairstyle looks and holds
- Leave a few **face-framing pieces** out if you want a softer and more romantic finish
- Avoid making the style too tight, or it may lose its soft effect
- Secure the style well with pins, even if the final look should appear light and effortless
- Let curls **cool fully** before brushing or loosening them
- Use a light mist of hairspray to hold the shape without making the hair stiff
- Keep a few essentials nearby, such as bobby pins, a comb, and a small finishing spray for touch-ups

Final Thought

Romantic soft styles are all about creating a bridal look that feels **soft, flattering, and timeless**. The right choice is not just the one that looks pretty in a picture, but the one that suits your hair, your comfort, and your wedding style best. Choose a look that makes you feel beautiful, confident, and natural. **That is what makes it unforgettable.**

6. Loose Romantic Curls

Best for: Medium to long hair

Hair type: Straight, wavy, lightly curly

Skill level: Beginner

Time needed: 15 minutes

Best for: Ceremony, reception, garden weddings

Works with: Veil, floral pins, delicate tiaras

Hold level: Medium

Loose romantic curls are perfect for brides who want a soft, feminine, and effortless look. This hairstyle brings movement and elegance to the hair while still feeling relaxed and natural. It works beautifully for outdoor weddings, soft bridal makeup, and dresses with lace or flowing fabrics.

You'll Need

- Hairbrush or comb
- Curling iron or wand
- Heat protectant
- Hair clips for sectioning
- Hair spray
- Optional: floral clips, decorative pins, light serum

Before You Start

Make sure your hair is completely dry before curling. Apply heat protectant first, then section the hair so the curls are easier to create evenly. If your hair is very straight or heavy, use a light mousse or texture spray before styling for better hold.

Step-by-Step

Step 1: Brush your hair gently and divide it into small sections.

Step 2: Wrap each section around the curling iron, holding for a few seconds before releasing.

Step 3: Continue curling all sections, making sure the curls fall in a soft and natural direction.

Step 4: Let the curls cool fully before touching them so they hold their shape better.

Step 5: Gently loosen the curls with your fingers or a wide-tooth comb for a softer romantic finish.

Step 6: Set with hair spray and add a floral pin or delicate accessory if desired.

LOOSE ROMANTIC CURLS
6-STEP GUIDE

STEP 1

Brush your hair gently and divide it into small sections.

STEP 2

Wrap each section around the curling iron, holding for a few seconds before releasing.

STEP 3

Continue curling all sections, making sure the curls fall in a soft and natural direction.

STEP 4

Let the curls cool fully before touching them so they hold their shape better.

STEP 5

Gently loosen the curls with your fingers or a wide-tooth comb for a softer romantic finish.

STEP 6

Set with hair spray and add a floral pin or delicate accessory if desired.

Common Mistakes

- Curls fall flat too quickly
- Hair looks too stiff or overdone
- Curls clump together unevenly
- Ends look dry or frizzy

Quick Fixes

- Let curls cool completely before loosening them
- Use smaller sections if your hair does not hold curl well
- Separate curls gently with fingers, not a brush
- Smooth dry ends with a tiny amount of serum

Make It Your Own

- Sweep one side back with a decorative clip
- Add fresh flowers for a soft garden wedding look
- Pair with a side part for extra glamour

Heads-Up

Loose curls are simple to create, but they last much better when the hair is prepped well. Brides with very heavy or very straight hair may need stronger spray or tighter curls at the start so the final look stays soft but secure.

Loose romantic curls are a beautiful choice for brides who want softness, elegance, and movement all in one style.

7. Side-Swept Curls

Best for: Medium to long hair

    Hair type: Straight, wavy, curly

    Skill level: Beginner to intermediate

    Time needed: 15 minutes

    Best for: Reception, evening weddings, glamorous bridal looks

    Works with: Statement earrings, jeweled clips, side combs

    Hold level: Medium

Side-swept curls bring together romance and glamour in a very bridal way. By moving the curls to one side, the hairstyle frames the face beautifully and creates an elegant shape in photos. It is a great option for brides who want to highlight one shoulder, detailed necklines, or statement jewelery.

    You'll Need

- Hairbrush or comb

- Curling iron or wand
- Heat protectant
- Bobby pins
- Hair spray
- Optional: jeweled comb, decorative clip, light serum

Before You Start

Hair should be dry and lightly prepped with heat protectant. A deep side part often works best for this look, so decide which side flatters your face most before you begin.

Step-by-Step

Step 1: Create a deep side part and brush the hair smooth.

Step 2: Curl the hair in sections, focusing on soft, flowing curls rather than tight ringlets.

Step 3: Gather the curls gently toward one side, usually over the shoulder.

Step 4: Secure the opposite side discreetly with bobby pins behind the ear.

Step 5: Arrange the curls with your fingers so they fall softly and evenly over the shoulder.

Step 6: Finish with hair spray and place a decorative clip or comb on the pinned side if desired.

SIDE-SWEPT CURLS
6-STEP GUIDE

STEP 1

Create a deep side part and brush the hair smooth.

STEP 2

Curl the hair in sections, focusing on soft, flowing curls rather than tight ringlets.

STEP 3

Gather the curls gently toward one side, usually over the shoulder.

STEP 4

Secure the opposite side discreetly with bobby pins behind the ear.

STEP 5

Arrange the curls with your fingers so they fall softly and evenly over the shoulder.

STEP 6

Finish with hair spray and place a decorative or comb on the pinned side if desired.

Common Mistakes

- Hair slips back out of place
- Pinned side looks too flat
- Curls bunch too tightly on one shoulder
- Style feels unbalanced

Quick Fixes
- Use crossed bobby pins for stronger hold
- Lightly tease the pinned side before securing
- Spread curls gently with fingers for better shape
- Check symmetry in a mirror from the front and side

Make It Your Own
- Add a jeweled comb above the pinned section
- Leave a few soft strands around the face
- Pair with bold earrings for a glamorous finish

Heads-Up

This style photographs beautifully, but it works best when the pinned side is secure and clean. Brides with very thick hair may need a few extra pins hidden underneath to keep the style comfortably in place.

Side-swept curls are soft, flattering, and perfect for brides who want romance with a hint of red-carpet charm.

8. Floral Half-Up Waves

Best for: Medium to long hair

    Hair type: Straight, wavy, lightly curly

    Skill level: Beginner to intermediate

    Time needed: 10-15 minutes

    Best for: Ceremony, engagement, garden weddings, romantic weddings

    Works with: Floral pins, baby's breath, veil, pearl clips

    Hold level: Medium

Floral Half-Up Waves is a soft and dreamy bridal hairstyle that combines the beauty of loose flowing waves with the elegance of pinned-back detail. It is a lovely choice for brides who want their hair down but still want some shape and structure around the crown. The floral accents add a delicate bridal touch and make the hairstyle feel fresh, feminine, and wedding-ready.

    You'll Need

- Hairbrush or comb
- Curling iron or wand
- Heat protectant
- Bobby pins
- Small clear elastic
- Hair spray
- Optional: floral pins, baby's breath, pearl clips

Before You Start

This style works best on dry hair with soft waves or curls. If your hair is naturally straight, curl it first and let the curls cool before styling. A little texture spray or light mousse can help the waves hold better and give the pinned section more grip.

Step-by-Step

Step 1: Brush your hair gently and create soft waves throughout the mid-lengths and ends using a curling iron or wand.

Step 2: Take a small section from each side of your head above the ears and bring them toward the back.

Step 3: Twist each side section loosely for a softer look, then join them together at the back with a clear elastic or a few bobby pins.

Step 4: Gently tug the twisted sections a little to create softness and volume around the crown.

Step 5: Add floral pins, baby's breath, or a small decorative clip above the joined section to highlight the half-up detail.

Step 6: Finish with hair spray and lightly arrange the waves with your fingers for a soft romantic finish.

FLORAL HALF-UP WAVES

6-STEP GUIDE

STEP 1

Brush your hair gently and create soft waves throughout the mid-lengths and ends using a curling iron or wand.

STEP 2

Take a small section from each side of your head above the ears and bring them toward the back.

STEP 3

Twist each side section loosely for a softer look, then join them together at the back with a clear elastic or a few bobby pins.

STEP 4

Gently tug the twisted sections a little to create softness and volume around the crown.

STEP 5

Add floral pins, baby's breath, or a small decorative clip above the joined section to highlight the half-up detail.

STEP 6

Finish with hair spray and lightly arrange the waves with your fingers for a soft romantic finish.

Common Mistakes
- Waves fall flat too quickly
- The pinned section looks too tight
- Crown area looks flat
- Flowers do not stay in place

Quick Fixes
- Let curls cool fully before touching them
- Loosen the twists gently after pinning for a softer effect
- Lightly tease the crown before pinning the side sections
- Secure floral pieces with hidden bobby pins for extra hold

Make It Your Own
- Add baby's breath for a garden wedding feel
- Use pearl clips for a more classic bridal look
- Leave a few face-framing strands loose for extra softness
- Place a veil under the pinned section for a graceful finish

Heads-Up

This style is great for brides who want a natural and romantic look, but it usually holds best with a little prep and at least one practice run. If your hair is very fine or silky, use texture spray before styling so the twists and waves stay in place longer.

Floral Half-Up Waves is a beautiful choice when you want your hair to feel SOFT, ELEGANT, and full of bridal charm.

9. Romantic Braided Bun

Best for: Medium to long hair

    Hair type: Straight, wavy

    Skill level: Intermediate

    Time needed: 15 minutes

    Best for: Ceremony, reception, vintage or romantic weddings

    Works with: Veil, pearl pins, floral accents

    Hold level: Strong

A romantic braided bun adds texture and softness while still feeling secure enough for a full wedding day. The braid gives the style extra detail, and the bun keeps it polished and bridal. It is a beautiful choice for brides who want something elegant with a more handcrafted, textured finish.

    You'll Need

- Hairbrush or comb

- Hair elastic
- Bobby pins
- Hair spray
- Optional: curling iron, pearl pins, decorative comb

Before You Start

Hair with a little texture works best for this style. If your hair is very silky, use dry shampoo or texture spray first. Light waves can also help the braid and bun feel fuller.

Step-by-Step

Step 1: Brush your hair smooth and gather it into a low ponytail.

Step 2: Divide the ponytail into two sections and create a simple braid with one section.

Step 3: Twist the remaining loose section around the base of the ponytail to begin forming a bun.

Step 4: Wrap the braid around the bun, layering it neatly for added texture.

Step 5: Secure the bun and braid with bobby pins, checking that the shape feels balanced.

Step 6: Finish with hair spray and soften the style slightly by loosening a few face-framing strands.

ROMANTIC BRAIDED BUN
6-STEP GUIDE

STEP 1

Brush your hair smooth
and gather it into a low
ponytail.

STEP 2

Divide the ponytail into
two sections and create a
simple braid with one
section.

STEP 3

Twist the remaining loose
section around the base
of the ponytail to begin
forming a bun.

STEP 4

Wrap the braid around
the bun, layering it neatly
for added texture.

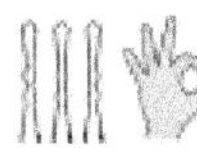

STEP 5

Secure the bun and braid
with bobby pins, checking
that the shape feels
balanced.

STEP 6

Finish with hair spray and
soften the style slightly by
loosening a few face–
framing strands.

Common Mistakes
- Braid looks too thin
- Bun shape feels messy instead of soft
- Pins show through the braid
- Style feels too tight

Quick Fixes
- Gently pull the braid apart before wrapping for more fullness
- Shape the bun first, then place the braid over it neatly
- Hide pins under the braid or inside the bun
- Loosen face-framing areas for a softer romantic look

Make It Your Own
- Add floral pins for a garden wedding feel
- Use pearl accents for a timeless bridal finish
- Keep a few strands loose near the face for softness

Heads-Up

This hairstyle is still simple, but it may take one or two practice runs to get the bun and braid balanced nicely. Brides with very layered hair may need extra pins to keep shorter pieces tucked in.

The romantic braided bun is elegant, textured, and perfect for brides who want softness with a little extra detail.

10. Pinned-Back Hollywood Waves

Best for: Medium to long hair

    Hair type: Straight, wavy, lightly curly

    Skill level: Beginner to intermediate

    Time needed: 15 minutes

    Best for: Ceremony, reception, glam weddings, evening events

    Works with: Side combs, pearl pins, crystal clips, veil

    Hold level: Medium

Pinned-Back Hollywood Waves bring together timeless glamour and soft bridal elegance. With smooth, polished waves and one or both sides pinned back, this hairstyle frames the face beautifully while keeping the look neat and camera-ready. It is a lovely choice for brides who want a romantic style that feels classic, feminine, and slightly vintage without looking too stiff.

    You'll Need

- Hairbrush or wide-tooth comb
- Curling iron or wand

- Heat protectant
- Bobby pins
- Hair spray
- Optional: shine serum, pearl pins, crystal clip, decorative comb

Before You Start

Start with dry hair and apply heat protectant before curling. This style works best when the waves are smooth and defined, so take time to brush the curls gently into shape after they cool. If your hair is very fine or soft, use a light mousse or texture spray first for better hold.

Step-by-Step

Step 1: Brush your hair and create a deep side part for a more classic Hollywood shape.

Step 2: Curl your hair in medium sections, turning each section in the same direction for smooth, flowing waves.

Step 3: Let the curls cool fully, then gently brush through them to create soft, even waves.

Step 4: Take a small section from the front or side and pin it neatly back above the ear, hiding the pin under the wave if possible.

Step 5: Adjust the front and sides with your fingers so the waves fall softly around the face and shoulders.

Step 6: Finish with hair spray and add a decorative clip, comb, or pins for a bridal touch.

PINNED-BACK HOLLYWOOD WAVES
6-STEP GUIDE

STEP 1

Brush your hair and create a deep side part for a more classic Hollywood shape.

STEP 2

Curl your hair in medium sections, turning each section in the same direction for smooth, flowing waves.

STEP 3

Let the curls cool fully, then gently brush through them to create soft, even waves.

STEP 4

Take a small section from the front or side and pin it neatly back above the ear, hiding the pin under the wave if possible.

STEP 5

Adjust the front and sides with your fingers so the waves fall softly around the face and shoulders.

STEP 6

Finish with hair spray and add a decorative clip, comb, or pins for a bridal touch.

Common Mistakes

- Waves look too tight instead of soft
- Hair becomes frizzy after brushing
- Pinned section looks too flat
- One side falls out too quickly

Quick Fixes

- Use larger curl sections for softer waves
- Wait until curls cool completely before brushing
- Gently lift the pinned section for a little more volume
- Secure the pinned area with two crossed bobby pins for better hold

Make It Your Own

- Add a crystal clip above the pinned section for a glam bridal finish
- Leave both sides softly pinned back for a more open face
- Place the veil underneath the pinned section for a cleaner look

Heads-Up

This style looks simple but the wave pattern matters. Practice once or twice to find the curl size and brushing technique that suits your hair best. Brides with very thick or heavy hair may need extra spray and pins to keep the waves polished for longer.

Pinned-Back Hollywood Waves are perfect for brides who want to look soft, elegant, and unforgettable.

Braided Bridal Looks

Braided bridal hairstyles are timeless, romantic, and versatile. They can look soft and effortless, polished and classic, or detailed and elegant depending on how they are styled. A braid can work beautifully for brides, bridesmaids, and even wedding guests because it adds texture, shape, and charm without always needing too much time or too many tools. Many braided looks also hold well through long ceremonies, outdoor settings, dancing, and photography, which makes them a practical choice for wedding events.

The best braided bridal hairstyle is the one that matches your hair type, comfort level, wedding vibe, and the amount of time you have to get ready. Some braided styles are quick and beginner-friendly, while others need more practice or a helping hand. Before choosing your look, think about how formal or relaxed you want your hairstyle to feel, whether you want to wear a veil or hair accessories, and how well your hair holds braids throughout the day. The right braid should not only look beautiful, but also feel secure, balanced, and easy enough to manage with confidence. **Choose beauty that lasts.**

How to choose the right braided bridal look

- Pick a braid style that matches your **hair length**. Longer hair can handle fuller braids, while short or layered hair often works better with side braids, crown details, or braided accents.
- Consider your **hair type and texture**. Thick hair can support bold and detailed braids, while fine hair may need teasing, texture spray, or looser braiding for a fuller look.
- Match the hairstyle to your **wedding theme**. Soft crown braids and loose side braids suit boho or garden weddings, while polished braided buns fit classic or formal weddings.
- Think about your **skill level**. Simple three-strand or side braids are easier for beginners, while fishtail, waterfall, or braided updos usually need more practice.
- Decide whether you want a **soft romantic look** or a more **neat and structured style**. Looser braids feel relaxed and dreamy, while tighter braids look cleaner and more defined.

- Check if the braid works well with your **veil, tiara, flowers, or hairpins**. Some styles leave better space for accessories than others.
- Consider the **weather and location**. Braids are often a smart choice for outdoor weddings because they hold shape better than loose curls in wind or humidity.
- Be honest about whether you will style it **yourself or with help**. Some braided looks are easy to do alone, but more detailed designs are easier with an extra pair of hands.
- Always choose a style that feels **comfortable and secure**, especially if you will wear it for many hours.
-

Braided bridal styling tips

- Start with hair that has a little **texture and grip**, since freshly washed silky hair can slip too easily.
- Use a light **texturizing spray or dry shampoo** before braiding to help the braid stay in place.
- Gently pull apart the braid after securing it if you want a **fuller, softer look**.
- Keep a few **bobby pins and clear elastics** nearby for quick fixes.
- Let a few face-framing strands loose if you want a more **romantic and effortless finish**.
- Practice the hairstyle at least **two or three times before the wedding day**.
- Take photos of your trial from the **front, side, and back** so you can see how it really looks.
- Test how the braid holds with your **accessories** before the big day.
- Finish with a flexible **hair spray** so the style stays secure without looking stiff.
- Have a simple **backup plan** in case your first braided choice takes too long or does not sit well with your hair.
- **Braids bring romance to bridal hair in the most timeless way.**

11. Braided Crown

Best for: Medium to long hair

Hair type: Straight, wavy, lightly curly

Skill level: Intermediate

Time needed: 15-20 minutes

Best for: Ceremony, garden weddings, boho weddings

Works with: Floral clips, baby's breath, delicate veil

Hold level: Medium to strong

The braided crown is a soft and romantic bridal hairstyle that wraps around the head like a halo. It gives a graceful, feminine look and works beautifully for outdoor, rustic, and bohemian weddings. Brides love this style because it feels elegant while still looking natural and relaxed.

You'll Need

- Hairbrush or comb

- Hair elastics
- Bobby pins
- Hair spray
- Optional: curling iron, fresh flowers, decorative pins

Before You Start

This hairstyle works best on dry hair with a little texture. If your hair is freshly washed, add a texturizing spray or dry shampoo first. Soft waves can also help the braid look fuller and more romantic.

Step-by-Step

Step 1: Brush your hair well and part it down the center or slightly to one side.

Step 2: Take a section near one ear and begin a braid, working along the hairline toward the back of the head.

Step 3: Repeat on the other side so you have two braids moving toward the back.

Step 4: Wrap each braid across the top or back of the head to create a crown effect.

Step 5: Secure the ends with bobby pins, tucking them neatly under the braid.

Step 6: Loosen the braid slightly for softness, then finish with hair spray and floral accents if desired.

BRAIDED CROWN
6-STEP GUIDE

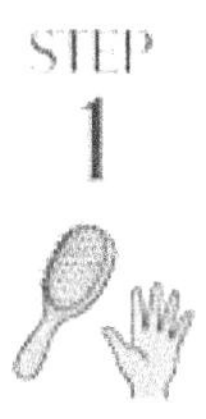 

STEP 1

Brush your hair well and part it down the center or slightly to one side.

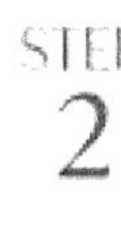  

STEP 2

Take a section near one ear and begin a braid, working along the hairline toward the back of the head.

STEP 3

Repeat on the other side so you have two braids moving toward the back.

STEP 4

Wrap each braid across the top or back of the head to create a crown effect.

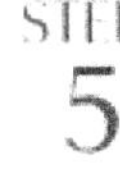  

STEP 5

Secure the ends with bobby pins, tucking them neatly under the braid.

STEP 6

Loosen the braid slightly for softness, then finish with hair spray and floral accents if desired.

Common Mistakes

- Braid looks too tight and stiff
- Crown sits unevenly
- Ends of the braid show
- Hair around the face feels too harsh

Quick Fixes

- Gently pull the braid wider with your fingers for a softer look
- Check both sides in a mirror before pinning fully
- Tuck braid ends under the fuller sections
- Pull out a few fine face-framing strands for softness

Make It Your Own

- Add tiny flowers for a garden wedding feel
- Use pearl pins for a classic bridal finish
- Pair with loose curls in the back for extra softness

Heads-Up

This style often looks best after a practice run because braid placement matters. Brides with thick hair may need extra pins to keep the crown secure all day.

The braided crown brings together romance, softness, and timeless bridal charm.

12. Side Braid Bridal Style

Best for: Medium to long hair

    Hair type: Straight, wavy, curly

    Skill level: Beginner

    Time needed: 10-15 minutes

    Best for: Beach weddings, boho weddings, bridesmaids

    Works with: Floral clips, jeweled pins, no veil or side veil

    Hold level: Medium

The side braid is an effortless bridal hairstyle that feels youthful, soft, and slightly playful. It falls over one shoulder and works especially well for brides who want a more relaxed look without losing elegance. This style is also a lovely choice for pre-wedding events and bridesmaids.

    You'll Need

- Hairbrush or comb

- Hair elastic
- Bobby pins
- Hair spray
- Optional: curling iron, flowers, ribbon

Before You Start

This style works beautifully with lightly curled or textured hair. If your hair is very silky, use a little mousse or texture spray first so the braid holds better.

Step-by-Step

Step 1: Brush your hair and sweep it all over one shoulder.

Step 2: Leave a few soft strands around the face if you want a romantic finish.

Step 3: Divide the hair into three sections and begin a loose braid over the shoulder.

Step 4: Continue braiding to the ends and secure with a small elastic.

Step 5: Gently pull at the braid to make it look fuller and softer.

Step 6: Set with hair spray and add floral or jeweled accents near the top if desired.

SIDE BRAID BRIDAL STYLE
6-STEP GUIDE

STEP 1

Brush your hair and sweep it all over one shoulder.

STEP 2

Leave a few soft strands around the face if you want a romantic finish.

STEP 3

Divide the hair into three sections and begin a loose braid over the shoulder.

STEP 4

Continue braiding to the ends and secure with a small elastic.

STEP 5

Gently pull at the braid to make it look fuller and softer.

STEP 6

Set with hair spray and add floral or jeweled accents near the top if desired.

Common Mistakes
- Braid looks too thin
- Hair slips out near the crown
- Style feels too casual
- Elastic at the end looks visible

Quick Fixes
- Pancake the braid gently to create fullness
- Add one or two hidden pins near the top
- Curl the front pieces for a more bridal finish
- Wrap a small strand of hair over the elastic

Make It Your Own
- Add baby's breath for a boho feel
- Pair with soft waves for extra volume
- Use a jeweled clip near the ear for elegance

Heads-Up

This is a great beginner-friendly style, but it works best when the braid is kept soft and full rather than tight. Fine hair may need teasing at the crown for better shape.

The side braid is simple, pretty, and perfect for brides who want soft beauty without too much structure.

13. Fishtail Bridal Braid

Best for: Medium to long hair

Hair type: Straight, wavy

Skill level: Intermediate

Time needed: 15-20 minutes

Best for: Boho weddings, beach weddings, engagement shoots

Works with: Floral accents, pearls, side clips

Hold level: Medium

The fishtail braid gives a bridal look that feels detailed, stylish, and slightly modern. It has a delicate woven appearance that stands out beautifully in photos. Brides who want something different from a classic braid often choose this look for its soft texture and visual interest.

You'll Need

• Hairbrush or comb

- Hair elastic
- Bobby pins
- Hair spray
- Optional: texturizing spray, decorative pins

Before You Start

This braid works best on hair with a little grip. Use texturizing spray if needed. Light waves can make the braid look fuller and more effortless.

Step-by-Step

Step 1: Brush your hair and gather it over one shoulder or at the back.

Step 2: Divide the hair into two large sections.

Step 3: Take a small piece from the outer edge of one section and cross it over into the other section.

Step 4: Repeat the same motion from side to side until you reach the ends.

Step 5: Secure the braid with an elastic and gently pull it wider for softness.

Step 6: Finish with hair spray and add decorative accents near the top or along the braid.

FISHTAIL BRIDAL BRAID
6-STEP GUIDE

STEP
1

Brush your hair and gather it over one shoulder or at the back.

STEP
2

Divide the hair into two large sections.

STEP
3

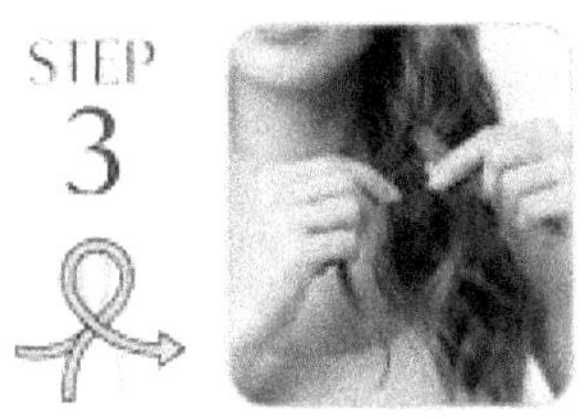

Take a small piece from the outer edge of one section and cross it over into the other section.

STEP
4

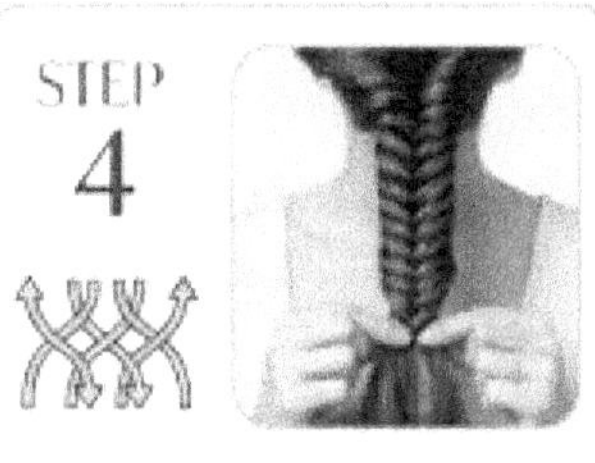

Repeat the same motion from side to side until you reach the ends.

STEP
5

Secure the braid with an elastic and gently pull it wider for softness.

STEP
6

Finish with hair spray and add decorative accents near the top or along the braid.

Common Mistakes

- Braid looks messy in the wrong way
- Sections are too big
- Braid feels loose too quickly
- Top of the style looks flat

Quick Fixes

- Keep the outer pieces smaller for a cleaner fishtail pattern
- Hold the braid firmly as you work
- Add a few pins near the top for support
- Tease the crown lightly before starting

Make It Your Own

- Wear it over one shoulder for a romantic feel
- Add tiny pearls through the braid
- Pair it with loose curled strands near the face

Heads-Up

This style can look tricky at first, so practice helps a lot. It is best for brides who like a textured look rather than a polished classic finish.

The fishtail braid is detailed, modern, and full of bridal personality.

14. Waterfall Braid with Curls

Best for: Medium to long hair

> **Hair type:** Straight, wavy, lightly curly
> **Skill level:** Intermediate
> **Time needed:** 15-20 minutes
> **Best for:** Ceremony, engagement party, romantic weddings
> **Works with:** Floral pins, jeweled combs, light veil
> **Hold level:** Medium

The waterfall braid with curls is soft, dreamy, and very bridal. The braid creates a lovely flowing pattern across the head while the rest of the hair falls in loose curls. It is perfect for brides who want a half-up style that feels graceful and feminine.

> **You'll Need**
> • Hairbrush or comb
> • Curling iron

- Bobby pins
- Hair spray
- Optional: decorative comb, flowers

Before You Start

Curl your hair lightly before braiding if you want a fuller and more polished finish. This hairstyle works best when the hair has movement and softness.

Step-by-Step

Step 1: Brush your hair and create soft curls through the lengths.

Step 2: Take a section near the front and begin a braid across the head.

Step 3: As you braid, drop one strand each time and pick up a new section to create the waterfall effect.

Step 4: Continue the braid until you reach the opposite side.

Step 5: Secure the end with a pin tucked under the hair.

Step 6: Adjust the curls, spray lightly, and add a decorative clip if desired.

ELEGANT WATERFALL
BRAID WITH CURLS
6-STEP GUIDE

STEP 1

Brush your hair and create soft curls through the lengths.

STEP 2

Take a section near the front and begin a braid across the head.

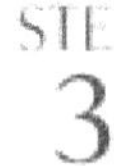
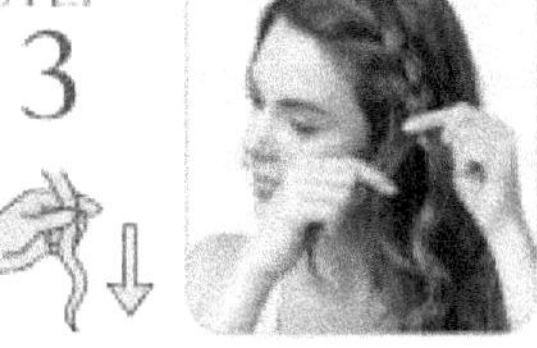
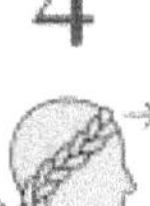

STEP 3

As you braid, drop one strand each time and pick up a new section to create the waterfall effect.

STEP 4

Continue the braid until you reach the opposite side.

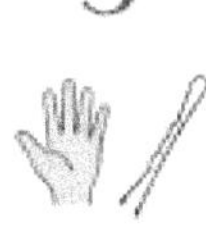

STEP 5

Secure the end with a pin tucked under the hair.

STEP 6

Adjust the curls, spray lightly, and add a decorative clip if desired.

Common Mistakes
- Waterfall strands do not fall neatly
- Braid looks uneven
- Curls drop too fast
- Pins show on the side

Quick Fixes
- Practice the braid pattern once before styling fully
- Work slowly and keep section sizes even
- Spray curls lightly before and after styling
- Hide pins under the top layer of hair

Make It Your Own
- Add soft flowers near the pinned side
- Make the curls looser for a beachy look
- Pair with a delicate side comb for extra shine

Heads-Up

This style is beautiful but needs a little coordination, so it is better after one or two trial runs. Very layered hair may need extra pinning to keep the braid looking neat.

The waterfall braid with curls is soft, romantic, and made for bridal photos.

15. Braided Low Bun

Best for: Medium to long hair

    Hair type: Straight, wavy, lightly curly

    Skill level: Intermediate

    Time needed: 15-20 minutes

    Best for: Ceremony, reception, elegant weddings

    Works with: Veil, pearl pins, decorative comb

    Hold level: Strong

The braided low bun combines the beauty of a braid with the timeless elegance of a bun. It creates texture and detail while still feeling polished and formal. This style is a wonderful choice for brides who want something classic with a little extra interest.

    You'll Need

- Hairbrush or comb

- Hair elastic
- Bobby pins
- Hair spray
- Optional: curling iron, pearl accessories

Before You Start

Add a little texture spray if your hair is soft or slippery. This style also looks beautiful with gently curled ends before you begin.

Step-by-Step

Step 1: Brush your hair and gather it into a low ponytail at the nape of your neck.

Step 2: Braid the ponytail loosely and secure the end with a small elastic.

Step 3: Wrap the braid around the base of the ponytail to form a bun.

Step 4: Secure the bun with bobby pins all around the shape.

Step 5: Pull out a few soft strands near the face if you want a romantic finish.

Step 6: Spray well and add pearl pins or a decorative comb if desired.

ELEGANT BRAIDED LOW BUN
6-STEP GUIDE

STEP 1

Brush your hair and gather it into a low ponytail at the nape of your neck.

STEP 2

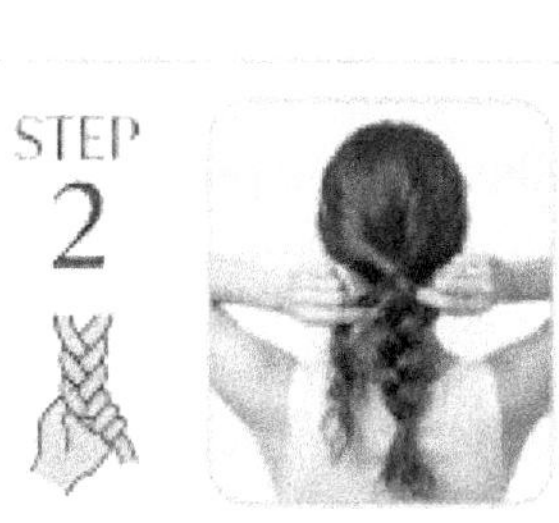

Braid the ponytail loosely and secure the end with a small elastic.

STEP 3

Wrap the braid around the base of the ponytail to form a bun.

STEP 4

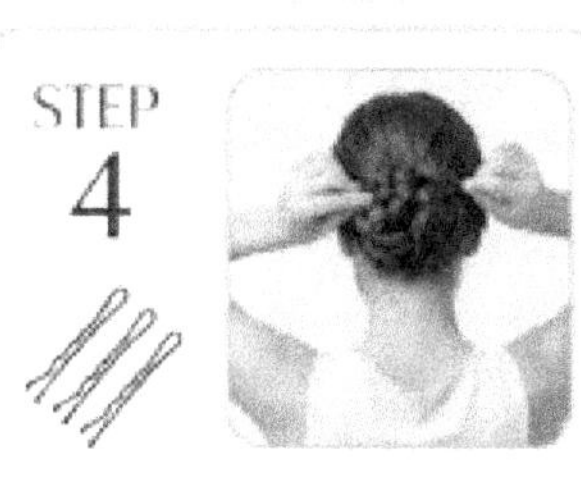

Secure the bun with bobby pins all around the shape.

STEP 5

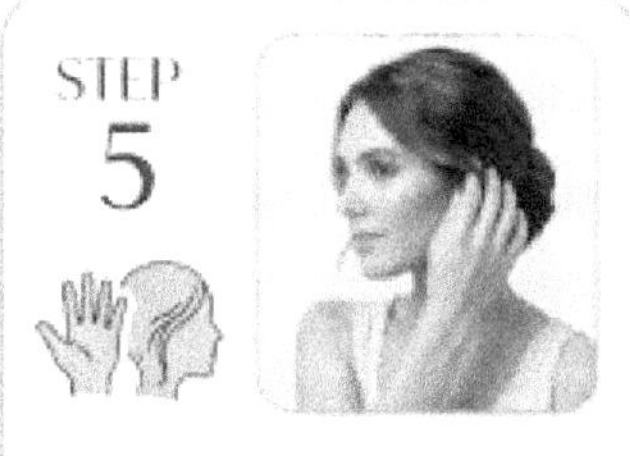

Pull out a few soft strands near the face if you want a romantic finish.

STEP 6

Spray well and add pearl pins or a decorative comb if desired.

Common Mistakes

- Bun looks too small or tight
- Braid untwists while wrapping
- Pins feel uncomfortable
- Crown looks flat

Quick Fixes

- Loosen the braid slightly before wrapping for more fullness
- Hold the braid firmly at the base as you pin
- Use smaller hidden pins instead of forcing large ones
- Tease the crown lightly before making the ponytail

Make It Your Own

- Add pearl pins for a timeless bridal finish
- Place the veil above the bun for a classic look
- Leave curled front pieces loose for softness

Heads-Up

This style usually lasts well, but brides with very layered hair may need extra pins at the bun edges. One practice run will help you find the best bun size and shape.

The braided low bun is elegant, secure, and beautifully bridal without feeling too plain.

Half-Up Hairstyles

Half-up hairstyles are perfect for brides who want a look that feels **romantic, balanced, and easy to wear**. They combine the best of both worlds: the elegance of an updo and the softness of loose hair. This style works especially well for weddings because it helps frame the face beautifully while keeping hair away from the eyes and off the cheeks.

Another reason half-up hairstyles are so popular is their flexibility. They can look **classic, boho, modern, soft, or glamorous** depending on how you style them. You can add braids, twists, curls, volume at the crown, or delicate accessories to match your dress, theme, and personal taste. They also work well for many hair lengths and textures, which makes them a reliable choice for brides, bridesmaids, and wedding guests alike.

How to Choose the Right Half-Up Hairstyle

- Choose a **soft curled half-up style** if you want a romantic and timeless bridal look.
- Pick a **twisted half-up hairstyle** if you want something elegant and simple.
- Go for a **braided half-up look** if your wedding has a boho, rustic, or outdoor feel.
- Select a style with **volume at the crown** if you want a more formal and flattering shape.
- Choose a **sleeker half-up look** if your dress and overall styling are modern or minimal.
- If you have **fine hair**, pick styles that include curls, teasing, or texture for fuller-looking volume.
- If you have **thick hair**, choose styles that control bulk while still showing off your length.
- If you have **shorter hair**, go for simpler half-up styles with twists, mini braids, or pinned-back sections.
- If you plan to wear a **veil**, choose a half-up style that leaves enough secure space for pinning it in place.
- If you want to style your hair yourself, choose a half-up look that uses

fewer sections, fewer pins, and simple steps.

Tips for Getting the Best Results

- Start with **dry, well-prepped hair** for better hold and easier styling.
- Add **light texture spray or dry shampoo** if your hair is too soft or slippery.
- Curl the loose sections first if you want extra softness and body.
- Gently tease the crown if you want more volume and a better shape.
- Keep both sides even when pulling hair back to avoid an unbalanced look.
- Use a mirror to check the style from the **front, side, and back**.
- Secure the half-up section well, because loose top sections can drop during the day.
- Hide bobby pins neatly under twists, braids, or lifted sections of hair.
- Do a full **practice run** before the wedding day to test comfort, hold, and appearance.
- Take photos in natural light to see how the hairstyle will look in pictures.
- Avoid using too many accessories if the hairstyle already has braids, curls, or twists.
- Finish with a **light but reliable hairspray** so the style stays soft, not stiff.

Final Thought

Half-up hairstyles are a beautiful choice when you want something that feels **ELEGANT, SOFT, and WEARABLE**. With the right style, a little preparation, and a few smart finishing touches, you can create a look that feels bridal without feeling overdone.

A great half-up hairstyle should feel like you just more polished for the big day.

16. Classic Half-Up Twist

Best for: Medium to long hair

Hair type: Straight, wavy, lightly curly

Skill level: Beginner

Time needed: 10-15 minutes

Best for: Ceremony, reception, classic and romantic weddings

Works with: Veil, pearl pins, floral clips

Hold level: Medium

The classic half-up twist is one of the easiest and most elegant bridal hairstyles to create. It gently pulls hair away from the face while keeping the rest soft and flowing. This style suits brides who want a graceful look that feels polished without looking too formal.

You'll Need

- Hairbrush or comb

- Bobby pins
- Small clear elastic
- Hair spray
- Optional: curling iron, pearl pins, decorative clip

Before You Start

Start with dry hair that has light texture. Soft waves work especially well for this hairstyle because they add movement and make the twist look fuller. If your hair is very smooth, use a little texture spray before styling.

Step-by-Step

Step 1: Brush your hair and create soft curls or waves if you want extra volume and texture.

Step 2: Take a section of hair from one side near the temple and twist it gently toward the back of your head.

Step 3: Repeat on the other side, bringing both twisted sections together at the back.

Step 4: Secure the two sections together with a clear elastic or bobby pins.

Step 5: Gently loosen the twists with your fingers to make them look softer and fuller.

Step 6: Finish with hair spray and add pearl pins or a decorative clip if desired.

CLASSIC HALF-UP TWIST
6-STEP GUIDE

STEP
1

Brush your hair and
create soft curls or waves
if you want extra
volume and texture.

STEP
2

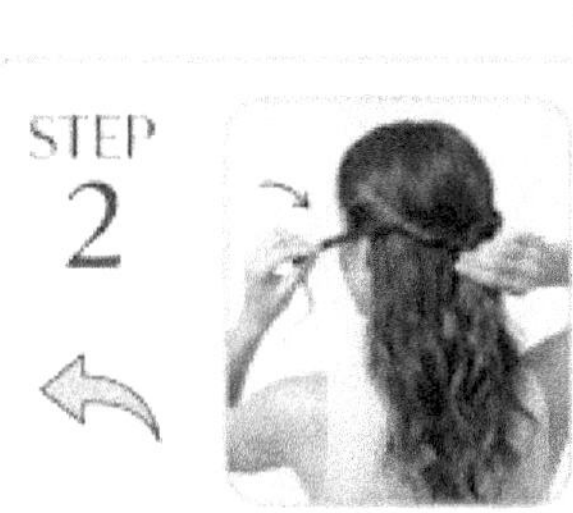

Take a section of hair from
one side near the temple
and twist it gently toward
the back of your head.

STEP
3

Repeat on the other side,
bringing both twisted
sections together at the
back.

STEP
4

Secure the two sections
together with a clear
elastic or bobby pins.

STEP
5

Gently loosen the twists
with your fingers to make
them look softer and fuller.

STEP
6

Finish with hair spray
and add pearl pins or a
decorative clip if desired.

Common Mistakes
- Twists look too tight and stiff
- Hair at the crown falls flat
- Twists slide down after a while
- Both sides do not look even

Quick Fixes
- Gently pull the twists wider after pinning
- Tease the crown lightly before styling
- Use crossed bobby pins for stronger hold
- Check both sides in a mirror before final spray

Make It Your Own
- Add pearl pins for a classic bridal feel
- Curl the loose hair for a romantic finish
- Use a floral clip for a garden wedding look

Heads-Up

This style is beginner-friendly and very wearable, but it looks best when both sides are balanced well. A quick practice run will help you make the twists more even and polished.

The classic half-up twist is simple, soft, and timeless in the most effortless way.

17. Half-Up Braided Crown

Best for: Medium to long hair

    Hair type: Straight, wavy, lightly curly

    Skill level: Intermediate

    Time needed: 15 minutes

    Best for: Outdoor weddings, boho weddings, romantic ceremonies

    Works with: Fresh flowers, baby's breath, vine accessories

    Hold level: Medium

The half-up braided crown adds charm and detail without being too heavy. It frames the head beautifully and gives a soft bridal shape while leaving the rest of the hair loose. This hairstyle is perfect for brides who want a natural, dreamy, and feminine look.

    You'll Need

- Hairbrush or comb

- Bobby pins
- Small clear elastics
- Hair spray
- Optional: curling iron, floral pins, hair vine

Before You Start

This style works best on hair with a bit of grip. If your hair is very silky, use dry shampoo or texture spray before braiding. Light waves can make the finished style look fuller and more romantic.

Step-by-Step

Step 1: Brush your hair and add soft waves if desired.

Step 2: Take a section of hair from one side near the temple and create a simple braid. Secure the end with a small elastic.

Step 3: Repeat on the other side with a matching braid.

Step 4: Bring both braids toward the back of your head, crossing them slightly if needed for a crown effect.

Step 5: Pin the braids securely in place and hide the ends underneath the opposite braid or loose hair.

Step 6: Loosen the braids gently for a softer look, then finish with spray and floral accents if desired.

HALF-UP BRAIDED CROWN
6-STEP GUIDE

STEP 1

Brush your hair and add soft waves if desired.

STEP 2

Take a section of hair from one side near the temple and create a simple braid. Secure the end with a small elastic.

STEP 3

Repeat on the other side with a matching braid.

STEP 4

Bring both braids toward the back of your head, crossing them slightly if needed for a crown effect.

STEP 5

Pin the braids securely in place and hide the ends underneath the opposite braid or loose hair.

STEP 6

Loosen the braids gently for a softer look, then finish with spray and floral accents if desired.

Common Mistakes
- Braids look too thin
- Braids sit too low and lose the crown shape
- Ends of the braid show too much
- Hair looks flat around the top

Quick Fixes
- Pull the braid loops slightly wider for fullness
- Position braids a little higher before pinning
- Tuck braid ends carefully under the loose hair
- Add light volume at the crown before starting

Make It Your Own
- Add baby's breath for a soft garden feel
- Leave face-framing strands out for romance
- Pair with loose waves for extra bridal softness

Heads-Up

This hairstyle looks beautiful in photos, especially from the back and side. Brides with layered hair may need a few extra pins to keep small pieces secure.

The half-up braided crown feels gentle, romantic, and perfect for a bride who wants natural beauty with a special touch.

18. Half-Up Bouffant

Best for: Medium to long hair

    Hair type: Straight, wavy

    Skill level: Beginner to intermediate

    Time needed: 10-15 minutes

    Best for: Classic weddings, formal receptions, vintage-inspired looks

    Works with: Veil, comb accessories, crystal clips

    Hold level: Strong

The half-up bouffant is ideal for brides who want volume and elegance. With a softly lifted crown and flowing hair beneath, this hairstyle creates a graceful silhouette that looks polished and photogenic. It is especially flattering for brides who want a more structured bridal look.

    You'll Need

- Hairbrush or teasing comb

- Bobby pins
- Small elastic
- Hair spray
- Optional: curling iron, crystal clip, decorative comb

Before You Start

Dry hair works best for this style. If your hair is freshly washed and very soft, use a little dry shampoo before teasing. Light curls on the lower half can make the hairstyle feel softer and more bridal.

Step-by-Step

Step 1: Brush your hair and section off the top crown area.

Step 2: Gently tease the crown section underneath to create volume.

Step 3: Smooth the top layer over the teased section without flattening it.

Step 4: Gather the lifted crown section and pin or tie it at the back of your head.

Step 5: Adjust the height and shape with your fingers so it looks smooth and balanced.

Step 6: Set with hair spray and style the loose lengths in soft curls if desired.

HALF-UP BOUFFANT
6-STEP GUIDE

STEP 1

Brush your hair and section off the top crown area.

STEP 2

Gently tease the crown section underneath to create volume.

STEP 3

Smooth the top layer over the teased section without flattening it.

STEP 4

Gather the lifted crown section and pin or tie it at the back of your head.

STEP 5

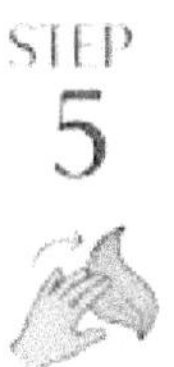

Adjust the height and shape with your fingers so it looks smooth and balanced.

STEP 6

Set with hair spray and style the loose lengths in soft curls if desired.

Common Mistakes
- Crown looks messy instead of smooth
- Volume falls flat too quickly
- Hair looks too stiff
- Back section sits crooked

Quick Fixes
- Tease only underneath and smooth only the top layer
- Use stronger spray at the roots before pinning
- Avoid over-brushing the top
- Check the center line in a mirror before finishing

Make It Your Own
- Add a crystal comb above the pinned section
- Pair with loose curls for a softer bridal finish
- Add a veil just below the half-up section

Heads-Up

This style gives beautiful height, but too much teasing can make it look dated. Keep the volume soft and elegant rather than overly dramatic.

The half-up bouffant brings a refined bridal shape that feels graceful, flattering, and timeless.

19. Curled Half-Up with Face-Framing Pieces

Best for: Medium to long hair

    Hair type: Straight, wavy, lightly curly

    Skill level: Beginner to intermediate

    Time needed: 10–15 minutes

    Best for: Ceremony, reception, romantic weddings

    Works with: Veil, pearl pins, floral clips, delicate combs

    Hold level: Medium

The curled half-up hairstyle with face-framing pieces is a soft and romantic bridal look that works beautifully for many wedding styles. It keeps the top section gently secured while allowing the rest of the hair to fall in soft curls, creating movement and elegance. The loose pieces around the face help soften the overall look and photograph beautifully from every angle.

    You'll Need

- Hairbrush or wide-tooth comb
- Curling iron or wand
- Heat protectant
- Bobby pins or a small clear elastic
- Hair spray
- Optional: pearl pins, floral clips, decorative comb

Before You Start

Start with dry hair and make sure it is fully brushed through. Apply heat protectant before curling. If your hair is very smooth or struggles to hold curls, use a light mousse, texture spray, or dry shampoo before styling. This will help the curls last longer and give the pinned section better grip.

Step-by-Step

Step 1: Brush your hair and curl it in medium sections, working away from the face for a soft bridal finish. Let the curls cool before touching them.

Step 2: Create a gentle center part or side part, depending on what suits your face best, and leave out two soft pieces near the front to frame the face.

Step 3: Take a section of hair from each side above the ears and bring them toward the back of your head.

Step 4: Twist each section lightly or simply smooth them back, then secure them together at the back with bobby pins or a small clear elastic.

Step 5: Gently loosen the pinned section a little for softness and adjust the face-framing pieces so they fall naturally around the cheeks or jawline.

Step 6: Finish with hair spray and add decorative pins or a small comb if you want an extra bridal touch.

CURLED HALF-UP WITH FACE-FRAMING PIECES
6-STEP GUIDE

STEP 1

Brush your hair and curl it in medium sections, working away from the face for a soft bridal finish. Let the curls cool before touching them.

STEP 2

PART

Create a gentle center part or side part, depending on what suits your face best, and leave out two soft pieces near the front to frame the face.

STEP 3

Take a section of hair from each side above the ears and bring them toward the back of your head.

STEP 4

Twist each section lightly or simply smooth them back, then secure them togethert the back with bobby pins or a small clear elastic.

STEP 5

adjust

Gently loosen the pinned section a little for softness and adjust the face-framing pieces so they fall naturally around the cheeks or jawline.

STEP 6

Finish with hair spray and add decorative pins or a small comb if you want an extra bridal touch.

Common Mistakes
- Curls fall flat too quickly
- Half-up section looks too tight or severe
- Face-framing pieces look uneven
- Pinned section slips down after a while

Quick Fixes
- Let curls cool fully before loosening them
- Gently pull the pinned section for a softer shape
- Use a mirror to check both front pieces for balance
- Cross two bobby pins for stronger hold at the back

Make It Your Own
- Add pearl pins for a classic bridal look
- Use floral clips for a garden or boho wedding
- Make the curls looser for a soft natural style or tighter for more glamour

Heads-Up

This hairstyle looks effortless, but it usually turns out best after one or two practice runs. If your hair is very heavy or very straight, use extra spray or a little teasing at the crown to help the half-up section stay secure.

The curled half-up style is perfect for brides who want a look that feels both polished and naturally romantic.

20. Half-Up Knot Style

Best for: Medium hair to long hair

    Hair type: Straight, wavy

    Skill level: Beginner

    Time needed: 10 minutes

    Best for: Minimal weddings, modern bridal looks, reception styling

    Works with: Sleek clips, pearl accessories, simple veils

    Hold level: Medium

The half-up knot style is modern, neat, and easy to create. It offers a fresh bridal option for those who want something simple yet stylish. This hairstyle feels less traditional than a twist or braid, making it a great choice for contemporary weddings.

    You'll Need

- Hairbrush or comb

- Small elastic
- Bobby pins
- Hair spray
- Optional: flat iron, sleek clip, pearl accessory

Before You Start

Smooth, frizz-free hair works best for this hairstyle. You can wear the loose hair straight, softly waved, or lightly curled depending on the overall bridal look you want.

Step-by-Step

Step 1: Brush your hair and smooth the top section neatly.

Step 2: Take the upper half of your hair from both sides and gather it at the back.

Step 3: Tie this section into a simple loose knot.

Step 4: Secure the knot with bobby pins and a small elastic if needed.

Step 5: Adjust the knot shape so it looks balanced and soft rather than tight.

Step 6: Finish with spray and add a simple clip or accessory if desired.

HALF-UP KNOT STYLE
6-STEP GUIDE

STEP 1

Brush your hair and smooth the top section neatly.

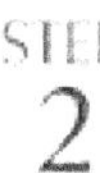

STEP 2

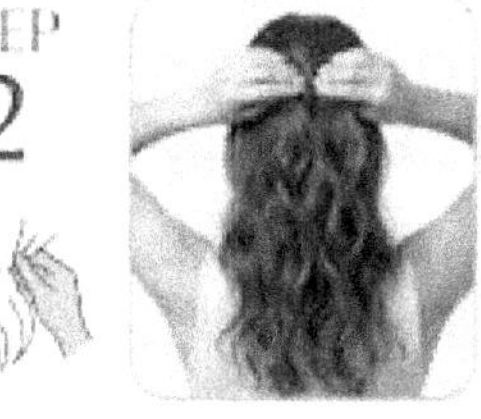

Take the upper half of your hair from both sides and gather it at the back.

STEP 3

Tie this section into a simple loose knot.

STEP 4

Secure the knot with bobby pins and a small elastic if needed.

STEP 5

Adjust the knot shape so it looks balanced and soft rather than tight.

STEP 6

Finish with spray and add a simple clip or accessory if desired.

Common Mistakes

- Knot becomes too tight and small
- Hair slips out after a short time
- Top looks flat and lifeless
- Knot sits off-center

Quick Fixes

- Keep the knot slightly loose before pinning
- Use pins underneath for hidden support
- Lift the crown lightly with fingers before spraying
- Center the knot carefully before final hold

Make It Your Own

- Add a pearl clip for bridal polish
- Curl the loose lengths for a romantic version
- Keep the hair sleek for a modern finish

Heads-Up

This style looks simple, but neat shaping makes all the difference. Practice once or twice so the knot looks intentional and elegant rather than casual.

The half-up knot style is perfect for brides who love clean beauty and understated elegance.

Short Hair Bridal Styles

Short hair bridal styles can be just as stunning as long hair looks. From soft waves and sleek bobs to pinned-back twists and delicate braided details, short hair offers many beautiful options for a wedding day. The right style can highlight your face, frame your neckline, and make your overall bridal look feel polished and complete. With the right prep, a few smart techniques, and well-chosen accessories, short hair can create a graceful style that feels timeless and special. **Short hair is not a limitation. It is a style advantage.**

How to choose the right short hair bridal style

- Choose a style that suits your **hair length** first, whether it is a pixie, bob, or shoulder-grazing cut.
- Work with your natural **hair texture** instead of fighting it. Straight, wavy, and curly hair each hold styles differently.
- Match the hairstyle to your **dress neckline** so the full bridal look feels balanced.
- Think about your **face shape** and choose volume, softness, or side details where they flatter you most.
- Pick a style that fits your **wedding theme**, such as classic, romantic, boho, beach, or modern.
- Decide whether you want a look that feels **soft and natural** or sleeker and more polished.
- Consider whether you will wear a **veil, tiara, comb, flowers, or clips**, since accessories can change which style works best.
- Be honest about your **skill level** if you are styling it yourself. Some short styles are much easier than others.
- Choose a style that can handle your **weather conditions**, especially if your wedding is outdoors.
- Always do a **trial run** before the wedding day to see how the style looks, feels, and lasts. **The best style is the one that truly works on your real hair.**

Tips for styling short bridal hair

- Start with clean hair that has a little grip, not hair that is too soft or slippery.
- Use **texture spray or dry shampoo** if your hair needs more hold.
- Do not overload short hair with heavy products, because it can make it flat.
- Add volume at the crown if you want a more bridal and balanced shape.
- Use small sections when curling or twisting for better control.
- Secure hidden areas well with bobby pins, especially near the back and sides.
- Leave a few soft face-framing pieces if you want a more romantic finish.
- Choose accessories that enhance the style, not overpower it.
- Check the hairstyle from the **front, side, and back** before finalizing it.
- Keep a few emergency items nearby, such as pins, a comb, and a mini hairspray.
- Practice the style more than once so you know how long it really takes.
- Take photos during your trial to see how the hairstyle appears on camera. **A beautiful bridal style should look good in person and in pictures.**

21. Soft Curled Bob

Best for: Short bob length hair

    Hair type: Straight, wavy

    Skill level: Beginner

    Time needed: 10-15 minutes

    Best for: Ceremony, reception, romantic weddings

    Works with: Veil, pearl clips, side combs

    Hold level: Medium

The soft curled bob is a beautiful choice for brides who want a feminine and polished look without putting their hair into an updo. Gentle curls add movement, softness, and volume, making short hair feel dressed up and wedding-ready. This style works especially well for brides who want elegance with a natural touch.

    You'll Need

- Hairbrush or comb
- Curling iron or straightener
- Heat protectant
- Bobby pins
- Hair spray
- Optional: pearl clip, floral pin, decorative side comb

Before You Start

Begin with dry hair and apply heat protectant before curling. If your hair is very fine or flat, use a little mousse or texture spray first to help the curls last longer and give the style more body.

Step-by-Step

Step 1: Brush your hair gently and create your preferred parting.

Step 2: Curl small to medium sections of hair away from the face for a soft bridal effect.

Step 3: Let the curls cool fully before touching them so they hold their shape better.

Step 4: Gently loosen the curls with your fingers or a wide-tooth comb for a softer finish.

Step 5: Pin one side back slightly if desired and add a decorative clip or comb.

Step 6: Finish with hair spray to hold the shape and reduce flyaway.

SOFT CURLED BOB
6-STEP GUIDE

STEP 1

Brush your hair gently and create your preferred parting.

STEP 2

Curl small to medium sections of hair away from the face for a soft bridal effect.

STEP 3

Let the curls cool fully before touching them so they hold their shape better.

STEP 4

Gently loosen the curls with your fingers or a wide-tooth comb for a softer finish.

STEP 5

Pin one side back slightly if desired and add a decorative clip or comb.

STEP 6

Finish with hair spray to hold the shape and reduce flyaways.

Common Mistakes

- Curls fall flat too quickly
- Hair looks too stiff
- One side looks fuller than the other
- Ends look frizzy

Quick Fixes

- Curl smaller sections for stronger hold
- Finger-comb instead of brushing too much
- Check both sides in the mirror before spraying
- Smooth the ends lightly with serum if needed

Make It Your Own

- Add a pearl clip on one side for a classic finish
- Use a deep side part for extra glamour
- Tuck one side behind the ear for a soft modern look

Heads-Up

This style is simple, but curl hold depends a lot on prep. Fine hair may need mousse or texture spray before styling for best results.

The soft curled bob is proof that short hair can look graceful, romantic, and fully bridal.

22. Twisted Side Pin Bridal Style

Best for: Short hair, bob length hair
    Hair type: Straight, wavy
    Skill level: Beginner
    Time needed: 8-12 minutes
    Best for: Ceremony, courthouse wedding, minimalist weddings
    Works with: Floral pins, pearl pins, delicate clips
    Hold level: Medium

The twisted side pin bridal style is ideal for brides who want something neat, soft, and easy without too much styling time. Small twists on one or both sides give the hairstyle detail and shape while keeping the overall look light and elegant. This is a great choice for modern brides who love simplicity.

    You'll Need
- Hairbrush or comb

- Bobby pins
- Hair spray
- Optional: pearl pins, floral clips, light texturizing spray

Before You Start

This style works best on dry hair with a little grip. If your hair is silky or freshly washed, use a small amount of dry shampoo or texture spray so the twists stay secure more easily.

Step-by-Step

Step 1: Brush your hair and create a center or side part depending on your preference.

Step 2: Take a small section from one front side and divide it into two pieces.

Step 3: Twist the two pieces backward, adding a little more hair as you move toward the ear.

Step 4: Pin the twist securely above or behind the ear.

Step 5: Repeat on the other side if you want a balanced look, or leave one side soft and open.

Step 6: Finish with hair spray and add pearl or floral pins if desired.

TWISTED SIDE PIN BRIDAL STYLE
6-STEP GUIDE FOR SHORT HAIR

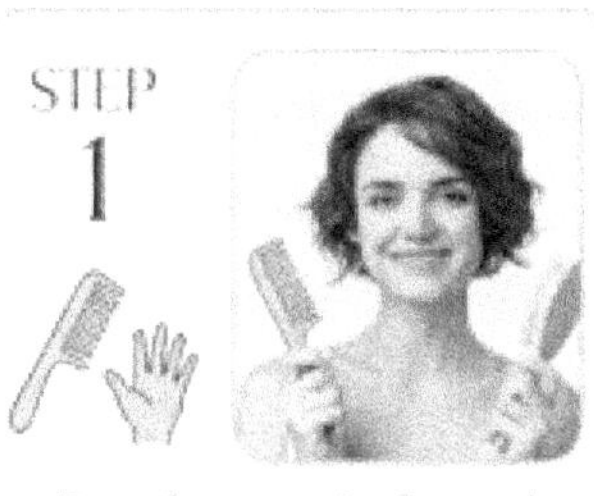

STEP 1

Brush your hair and create a center or side part depending on your preference.

STEP 2

Take a small section from one front side and divide it into two pieces.

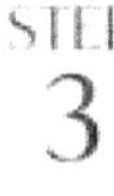

STEP 3

Twist the two pieces backward, adding a little more hair as you move toward the ear.

STEP 4

Pin the twist securely above or behind the ear.

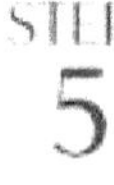

STEP 5

Repeat on the other side if you want a balanced look, or leave one side soft and open.

STEP 6

Finish with hair spray and add pearl or floral pins if desired.

Common Mistakes

- Twist comes loose quickly
- Front pieces stick out
- Pins become visible
- One side looks tighter than the other

Quick Fixes

- Twist firmly but not too tightly before pinning
- Smooth small flyaway with fingers and spray
- Hide pins under the twist line
- Compare both sides in the mirror before finishing

Make It Your Own

- Add tiny pearl pins along the twist
- Leave a few soft strands near the face
- Twist only one side for an asymmetrical modern look

Heads-Up

This style is easy, but symmetry matters. Practice once or twice so both sides look balanced if you plan to twist both.

The twisted side pin bridal style is delicate, wearable, and beautifully understated.

23. Crown Twist for Short Hair

Best for: Short hair, chin-length hair

    Hair type: Straight, wavy, lightly curly

    Skill level: Beginner to intermediate

    Time needed: 10-15 minutes

    Best for: Garden weddings, boho weddings, daytime ceremonies

    Works with: Floral pins, baby's breath, light veil

    Hold level: Medium

The crown twist for short hair gives a soft halo effect that feels romantic and bridal without needing long hair. It adds shape around the head and works especially well for outdoor or nature-inspired weddings. This style is ideal for brides who want something pretty, fresh, and slightly bohemian.

    You'll Need

- Hairbrush or comb

- Bobby pins
- Hair elastic if needed
- Hair spray
- Optional: floral pins, baby's breath, texturizing spray

Before You Start

Hair with a little texture usually works best for this look. If your hair is very soft or freshly washed, lightly curl the ends or use texture spray first to give the twists better hold.

Step-by-Step

Step 1: Part your hair in the center or slightly to one side.

Step 2: Take a small front section near the hairline and twist it backward toward the ear.

Step 3: Continue adding small pieces of hair into the twist as you move around the head.

Step 4: Pin the twist securely near the back of the head.

Step 5: Repeat the same on the other side and tuck the ends neatly where the twists meet.

Step 6: Finish with hair spray and add floral accents for a soft bridal touch.

CROWN TWIST FOR SHORT HAIR

6-STEP GUIDE

STEP 1: Part your hair in the center or slightly to one side.

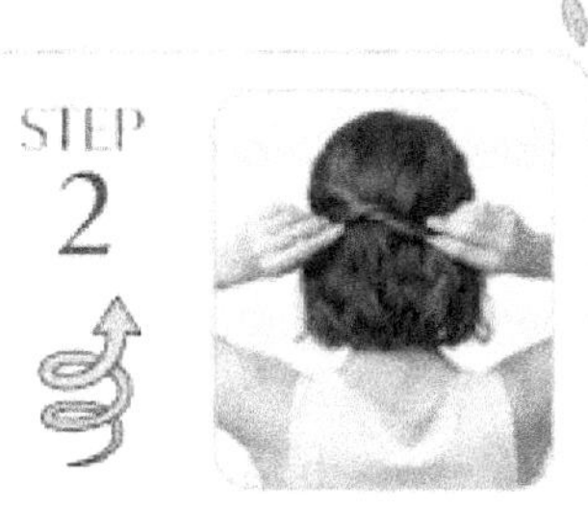

STEP 2: Take a small front section near the hairline and twist it backward toward the ear.

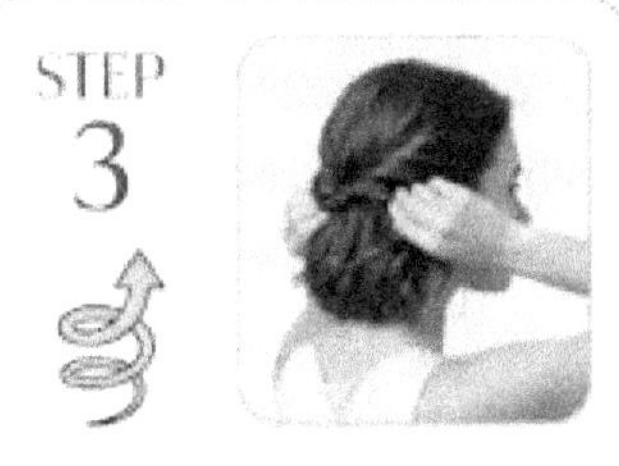

STEP 3: Continue adding small pieces of hair into the twist as you move around the head.

STEP 4: Pin the twist securely near the back of the head.

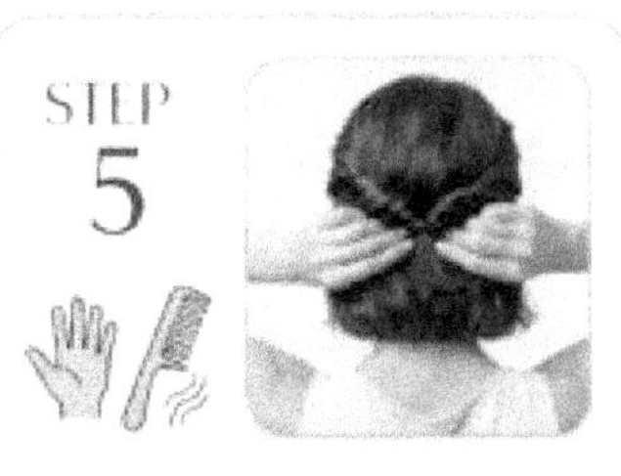

Repeat the same on the other side and tuck the ends neatly where the twists meet.

Finish with hair spray and add floral accents for a soft bridal touch.

Common Mistakes
- Twists look uneven
- Hair sticks out at the back
- Crown shape looks too flat
- Floral accents feel heavy

Quick Fixes
- Keep section sizes similar on both sides
- Tuck loose ends under the meeting point and pin well
- Gently lift the crown area with fingers before spraying
- Use small lightweight flowers instead of large clips

Make It Your Own
- Add baby's breath for a boho look
- Leave front strands loose for softness
- Place a light veil under the twist line at the back

Heads-Up

This style can take a little practice if you are new to twisting hair around the head. It is worth trying once before the big day to check balance and hold.

The crown twist for short hair feels dreamy, bridal, and effortlessly pretty.

24. Sleek Pinned Bob

Best for: Short bob or blunt-cut hair

    Hair type: Straight, slightly wavy

    Skill level: Beginner

    Time needed: 8-10 minutes

    Best for: Modern weddings, civil ceremonies, evening receptions

    Works with: Statement clips, jeweled pins, sleek veil

    Hold level: Strong

The sleek pinned bob is perfect for brides who want a clean, polished, and modern hairstyle. It brings attention to the face, earrings, neckline, and makeup while still feeling elegant enough for a wedding. This style is especially strong for minimalist brides who love a neat and refined finish.

    You'll Need

- Fine-tooth comb

- Smoothing serum or light gel
- Bobby pins
- Hair spray
- Optional: statement clip, jeweled barrette, sleek veil

Before You Start

Start with dry, smooth hair. If your hair tends to puff up, use a small amount of serum or smoothing cream before styling. This helps create the polished look that makes this style stand out.

Step-by-Step

Step 1: Brush your hair smooth and create a sharp center or side part.

Step 2: Apply a small amount of smoothing product through the top layers.

Step 3: Tuck one or both sides neatly behind the ears.

Step 4: Secure the tucked sections with hidden bobby pins or a decorative barrette.

Step 5: Smooth the top and sides gently with a comb for a clean finish.

Step 6: Set everything with hair spray to hold the sleek shape.

SLEEK PINNED BOB
6-STEP GUIDE FOR SHORT HAIR

STEP 1

Brush your hair smooth and create a sharp center or side part.

STEP 2

Apply a small amount of smoothing product through the top layers.

STEP 3

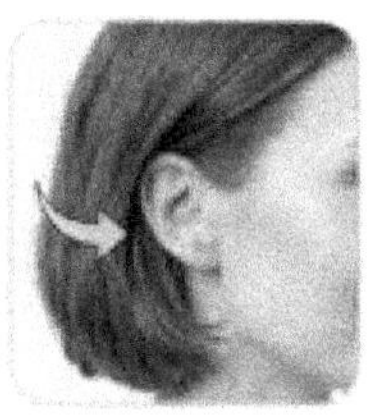

Tuck one or both sides neatly behind the ears.

STEP 4

Secure the tucked sections with hidden bobby pins or a decorative barrette.

STEP 5

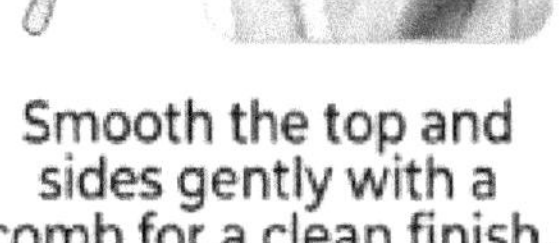

Smooth the top and sides gently with a comb for a clean finish.

STEP 6

Set everything with hair spray to hold the sleek shape.

Common Mistakes

- Hair looks greasy instead of sleek
- Tucked sides come loose
- Crown looks too flat
- Pins are too visible

Quick Fixes

- Use only a small amount of product
- Secure tucked sections with crossed pins
- Lift the crown very slightly before final spray if needed
- Place decorative clips over pin areas when possible

Make It Your Own

- Use a deep side part for stronger drama
- Add a jeweled barrette for a statement finish
- Pair with bold earrings for a modern bridal look

Heads-Up

This style looks best with clean lines, so take a little time to smooth the parting and sides well. Brides with very layered hair may need extra pins near the ears.

The sleek pinned bob is chic, confident, and beautifully modern for a wedding day.

25. Side-Swept Short Glam Waves

Best for: Short hair, chin-length to shoulder-length

    Hair type: Straight, wavy, lightly curly

    Skill level: Beginner to intermediate

    Time needed: 10–15 minutes

    Best for: Ceremony, reception, evening weddings, glam bridal looks

    Works with: Hair clips, crystal pins, side combs, mini veils

    Hold level: Medium

Side-swept short glam waves are a beautiful choice for brides who want a polished and elegant look without needing long hair or a full updo. This hairstyle creates soft volume, face-framing movement, and a red-carpet feel that works especially well for modern, vintage, or evening-inspired weddings. The deep side part adds drama, while the waves bring softness and shine.

    You'll Need

- Hairbrush or comb
- Curling iron or straightener
- Heat protectant
- Bobby pins
- Hair spray
- Optional: shine serum, crystal clip, decorative side comb

Before You Start

Start with dry hair and apply heat protectant before curling. If your hair is very clean and soft, use a little texture spray or light mousse first so the waves hold better. A deep side part works best for this style, so decide which side flatters your face most before you begin.

Step-by-Step

Step 1: Brush your hair gently and create a deep side part on the side you prefer.

Step 2: Curl small to medium sections of hair away from your face to create soft waves throughout.

Step 3: Let the curls cool for a minute, then gently loosen them with your fingers or a wide-tooth comb for a soft glam finish.

Step 4: Sweep the heavier side of your hair across the forehead and toward one side, allowing the waves to frame your face.

Step 5: Pin one side neatly above or behind the ear using bobby pins, and cover the pins with a decorative clip or comb if desired.

Step 6: Finish with hair spray to hold the waves in place and smooth a tiny amount of shine serum over the ends if needed.

SIDE-SWEPT SHORT GLAM WAVES

6-STEP GUIDE

STEP 1

Brush your hair gently and create a deep side part on the side you prefer.

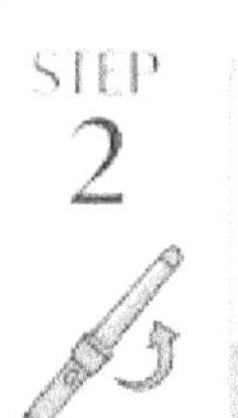

STEP 2

Curl small to medium sections of hair away from your face to create soft waves throughout.

STEP 3

Let the curls cool for a minute, then gently loosen them with your fingers or a wide-tooth comb for a soft glam finish.

STEP 4

Sweep the heavier side of your hair across the forehead and toward one side, allowing the waves to frame your face.

STEP 5

Pin one side neatly above or behind the ear using bobby pins, and cover the pins with a decorative clip or comb if desired.

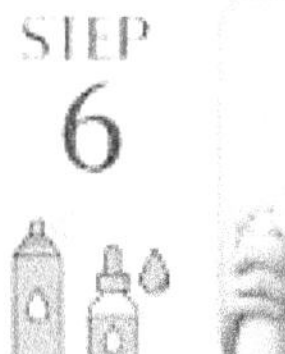
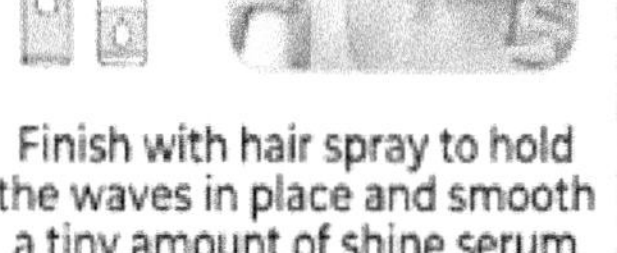

STEP 6

Finish with hair spray to hold the waves in place and smooth a tiny amount of shine serum over the ends if needed.

Common Mistakes

- Waves look too tight instead of soft
- Hair falls flat on the pinned side
- The side part does not stay in place
- Ends look frizzy or dry

Quick Fixes

- Gently brush or finger-comb the curls to soften them
- Use two crossed bobby pins for better hold on the pinned side
- Add a little hair spray along the parting line before setting it
- Smooth a small drop of serum over the ends for a neater finish

Make It Your Own

- Add a crystal clip for a glamorous bridal touch
- Tuck one side behind the ear for a cleaner look
- Keep a few soft strands near the face for a romantic finish

Heads-Up

This hairstyle works best when the curls are allowed to cool before touching them. If your hair is very fine or straight, you may need extra spray or a bit of texture product to help the waves last longer. A short trial run will help you find the best side part and wave shape for your face.

Side-swept short glam waves are perfect for brides who want to prove that short hair can look every bit as elegant, soft, and wedding-ready as any classic bridal style.

Quick Bridesmaid and Guest Styles

Need a quick, elegant style without the stress? This section is for bridesmaids and wedding guests who want a hairstyle that looks polished, feels comfortable, and can be done without spending hours in front of the mirror.

Unlike the bride's hairstyle, bridesmaid and guest styles should support the overall wedding look without pulling too much attention. The best choice is one that matches the event, works with your hair type, stays in place for hours, and feels like **YOU**. A beautiful hairstyle is not just about how it looks in the first 10 minutes. It should still look good through photos, movement, weather, and celebration. **That is the goal.**

How to Choose the Right Bridesmaid or Guest Hairstyle

- **Match the formality of the event**
  A black-tie evening wedding may suit sleek buns, soft chignons, or polished curls. A beach or garden wedding may look better with loose waves, braided styles, or soft half-up looks.
- **Think about your role in the wedding**
  Bridesmaids usually need a hairstyle that looks neat, lasts longer, and fits the group aesthetic. Guests can often choose something more personal and flexible.
- **Choose based on your hair length**
  Short hair works well with side twists, pinned waves, or mini braided accents. Medium hair is great for low buns, half-up styles, and soft curls. Long hair gives more room for braids, updos, and fuller styles.
- **Work with your natural hair texture**
  Straight hair suits sleek and modern looks. Wavy hair is ideal for romantic and soft styles. Curly hair works beautifully in textured updos, half-up styles, and natural volume looks.
- **Consider the weather and location**
  Outdoor, windy, or humid weddings need more secure hairstyles. Loose curls may fall quickly in humidity, while buns, braids, and pinned styles usually last longer.
- **Match the hairstyle to your outfit neckline**

Off-shoulder, halter, and high-neck outfits often look better with hair up or partly up. Open necklines work well with soft curls, side-swept styles, or loose half-up looks.

- **Be realistic about your skill level**
  If you are styling your own hair, choose a look you can actually do with confidence. A simple, clean hairstyle is better than a complicated one that falls apart.
- **Think about comfort for the full day**
  Avoid styles that feel too tight, heavy, or full of pins if you will be wearing them for many hours.
- **Choose a style that photographs well from all angles**
  Wedding photos are taken from the front, side, and back. Pick a style that looks balanced from every view.
- **Do a trial if the event matters a lot**
  Even a quick 10-minute practice can help you avoid surprises and save time on the day. **Preparation creates confidence.**

Quick Tips for Bridesmaid and Guest Hairstyles

- Pick a style that takes **less time than you think you need**
- Start with clean, fully dry, and detangled hair
- Use light product before styling if your hair is slippery or too soft
- Keep extra pins, elastics, and a mini hair spray nearby
- Secure the style well, especially if you will dance or stay long hours
- Leave a few soft face-framing pieces only if they suit your face shape
- Do not overload the hairstyle with too many accessories
- If the dress is detailed, keep the hair simpler
- If the dress is simple, the hairstyle can have a little more texture or detail
- Choose comfort over trend if you are unsure
- For group styling, keep the overall look coordinated, not necessarily identical
- Always check the hairstyle in natural light before leaving
- Take one front photo, one side photo, and one back photo after styling

- Have a backup plan in case curls drop or pins loosen
- When in doubt, choose a low bun, soft curls, or a half-up style-they are usually the safest and most flattering options

149

26. Quick Low Ponytail Twist

Best for: Medium to long hair

Hair type: Straight, wavy, lightly curly

Skill level: Beginner

Time needed: 8–12 minutes

Best for: Bridesmaids, wedding guests, rehearsal dinners, simple receptions

Works with: Pearl pins, floral clips, soft veils, decorative combs

Hold level: Medium

The quick low ponytail twist is a soft and polished hairstyle that feels elegant without looking overdone. It sits neatly at the nape of the neck and works beautifully for bridesmaids or guests who want something graceful, easy, and comfortable to wear for hours. This style is especially helpful when you want a neat finish with very little effort.

You'll Need

- Hairbrush or comb
- Hair elastic
- Bobby pins

- Hair spray
- Optional: curling iron, pearl pins, decorative clip

Before You Start

This hairstyle works best on dry hair with a little grip. If your hair is freshly washed and very smooth, use a light texture spray or dry shampoo first. This helps the twisted sections stay in place and gives the ponytail a fuller look.

Step-by-Step

Step 1: Brush your hair gently to remove tangles and create a clean, smooth base.

Step 2: Take one section from each side of your head, twist them loosely toward the back, and bring them together at the nape.

Step 3: Secure the twisted sections with an elastic along with the rest of your hair to form a low ponytail.

Step 4: Gently tighten and adjust the twists so they look even and soft.

Step 5: Wrap a small piece of hair around the elastic to hide it, then pin it underneath.

Step 6: Finish with hair spray and add a decorative pin or clip if desired.

QUICK LOW PONYTAIL TWIST

STEP 1

Brush your hair gently to remove tangles and create a clean, smooth base.

STEP 2

Take one section from each side of your head, twist them loosely toward the back, and bring them together at the nape.

STEP 3

Secure the twisted sections with an elastic along with the rest of your hair to form a low ponytail.

STEP 4

Gently tighten and adjust the twists so they look even and soft.

STEP 5

Wrap a small piece of hair around the elastic to hide it, then pin it underneath.

STEP 6

Finish with hair spray and add a decorative pin or clip if desired.

Common Mistakes
- Twists look uneven on both sides
- Ponytail feels too flat
- Elastic shows too much
- Side sections become loose

Quick Fixes
- Check both twists in a mirror before securing them
- Gently tease the crown or ponytail for extra fullness
- Wrap a strand of hair around the elastic for a neater finish
- Add one hidden bobby pin under each twist for stronger hold

Make It Your Own
- Curl the ponytail ends for a softer finish
- Add pearl pins where the twists meet
- Leave a few face-framing strands out for a romantic look

Heads-Up

This style is simple, but the balance of the twists matters. Take a moment to check both sides before finishing. If your hair is heavily layered, a few extra pins may help keep shorter pieces in place.

The quick low ponytail twist is a lovely reminder that soft elegance can be created in just minutes.

27. Side-Swept Ponytail Curls

Best for: Medium to long hair

    Hair type: Straight, wavy, curly

    Skill level: Beginner to intermediate

    Time needed: 10–15 minutes

    Best for: Bridesmaids, wedding guests, receptions, romantic weddings

    Works with: Floral clips, jeweled pins, soft curls, side accessories

    Hold level: Medium

The side-swept ponytail curls style is feminine, graceful, and full of movement. Worn over one shoulder, it creates a soft romantic look that works especially well for weddings and evening events. It is a great choice for anyone who wants the beauty of curls without the effort of a full updo.

    You'll Need

- Hairbrush or wide-tooth comb

- Hair elastic
- Bobby pins
- Curling iron
- Hair spray
- Optional: decorative side clip, serum for shine

Before You Start

This hairstyle looks best when the hair has loose curls or soft waves. If your hair is naturally straight, curl it lightly before styling. Let the curls cool first so they hold better and keep their shape longer.

Step-by-Step

Step 1: Curl your hair in medium sections and let the curls cool completely before touching them.

Step 2: Sweep all your hair gently to one side and gather it just below the ear into a low side ponytail.

Step 3: Secure the ponytail with an elastic, keeping the top soft rather than too tight.

Step 4: Loosen a few small sections near the crown and around the face for a softer finish.

Step 5: Twist or wrap a small strand of hair around the elastic and pin it underneath to hide it.

Step 6: Set the style with hair spray and arrange the curls over the shoulder for a smooth, full look.

SIDE-SWEPT PONYTAIL CURLS
6-STEP GUIDE

STEP 1

Curl your hair in medium sections and let the curls cool completely before touching them.

STEP 2

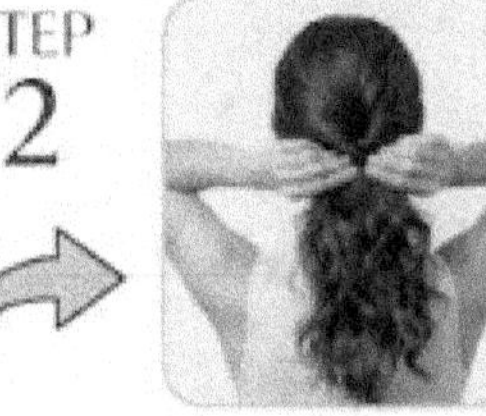

Sweep all your hair gently to one side and gather it just below the ear into a low side ponytail.

STEP 3

Secure the ponytail with an elastic, keeping the top soft rather than too tight.

STEP 4

Loosen a few small sections near the crown and around the face for a softer finish.

STEP 5

Twist or wrap a small strand of hair around the elastic and pin it underneath to hide it.

STEP 6

Set the style with hair spray and arrange the curls over the shoulder for a smooth, full look.

Common Mistakes
- Curls lose shape too quickly
- Ponytail slips backward
- Top looks too flat
- Side ponytail feels too tight

Quick Fixes
- Spray each curl lightly before gathering the ponytail
- Use bobby pins above the ponytail base for extra support
- Loosen the crown gently with your fingers
- Keep the ponytail soft so it feels romantic, not stiff

Make It Your Own
- Add a jeweled clip above the ponytail
- Leave side bangs or face-framing strands loose
- Use tighter curls for a more glamorous look

Heads-Up

If your hair is very thick or heavy, this side ponytail may need a few hidden pins for support. Practice once before the event so you can see which side feels and looks best on you.

The side-swept ponytail curls style is soft, flattering, and perfect when you want romance without too much structure.

28. Easy Textured Low Bun

Best for: Medium to long hair

Hair type: Straight, wavy, curly

Skill level: Beginner

Time needed: 10–15 minutes

Best for: Bridesmaids, wedding guests, garden weddings, classic and romantic events

Works with: Floral pins, pearl clips, decorative combs, soft veils

Hold level: Medium to strong

The easy textured low bun is one of the most versatile styles for wedding events. It has a relaxed and slightly undone feel, yet still looks polished and elegant. This makes it perfect for bridesmaids and guests who want a hairstyle that feels soft, modern, and easy to wear from day to night.

You'll Need

- Hairbrush or comb
- Hair elastic

- Bobby pins
- Texture spray or dry shampoo
- Hair spray
- Optional: curling iron, decorative pins

Before You Start

For the best textured finish, do not make the hair too smooth. Use dry hair with light texture spray or dry shampoo to create grip and fullness. If you want extra softness, curl a few sections before styling.

Step-by-Step

Step 1: Brush your hair lightly and apply texture spray through the mid-lengths and roots.

Step 2: Gather your hair into a low ponytail at the nape, keeping the top soft and natural.

Step 3: Twist the ponytail loosely and wrap it around the base to create a relaxed bun.

Step 4: Secure the bun with bobby pins, letting a little texture show instead of making it too perfect.

Step 5: Gently pull at small sections around the crown and near the bun to create softness and volume.

Step 6: Finish with hair spray and add decorative pins if desired.

EASY TEXTURED LOW BUN
6-STEP GUIDE

STEP 1

Brush your hair lightly and apply texture spray through the mid-lengths and roots.

STEP 2

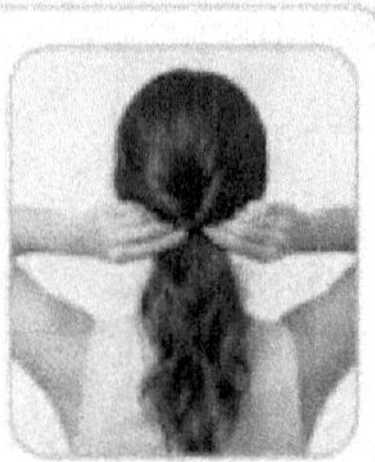

Gather your hair into a low ponytail at the nape, keeping the top soft and natural.

STEP 3

Twist the ponytail loosely and wrap it around the base to create a relaxed bun.

STEP 4

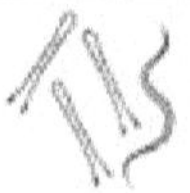

Secure the bun with bobby pins, letting a little texture show instead of making it too perfect.

STEP 5

Gently pull at small sections around the crown and near the bun to create softness and volume.

STEP 6

Finish with hair spray and add decorative pins if desired.

Common Mistakes
- Bun looks too tight or too plain
- Crown has no volume
- Bun starts coming loose
- Too many flyaway appear

Quick Fixes
- Loosen the bun slightly with your fingers after pinning
- Tease the crown lightly before making the ponytail
- Use crossed bobby pins around the bun base
- Smooth only the top layer so the style keeps its texture

Make It Your Own
- Add floral pins for a garden wedding feel
- Leave soft tendrils around the face
- Curl a few front sections for extra romance

Heads-Up

This style looks best when it is not too perfect. A little softness makes it more flattering and modern. If your hair is very silky, use extra texture spray before starting.

The easy textured low bun is effortless beauty at its best-soft, pretty, and made for special moments.

29. Simple Braided Ponytail

Best for: Medium to long hair

    Hair type: Straight, wavy, lightly curly

    Skill level: Beginner

    Time needed: 8–12 minutes

    Best for: Bridesmaids, wedding guests, casual weddings, outdoor events

    Works with: Ribbon, pearl pins, floral clips, decorative elastics

    Hold level: Medium to strong

The simple braided ponytail is a charming style that combines neatness with just the right amount of detail. It is easy to create, stays in place well, and works beautifully for daytime weddings or relaxed celebrations. This hairstyle is ideal for anyone who wants something youthful, secure, and elegant without too much effort.

    You'll Need

- Hairbrush or comb
- Hair elastic
- Small clear elastic
- Hair spray
- Optional: ribbon, decorative clip, texture spray

Before You Start

This style works best on smooth but not overly slippery hair. If your hair is very soft, a little texture spray can help the braid hold better. Brush the hair well first so the braid looks neat and even.

Step-by-Step

Step 1: Brush your hair smoothly and gather it into a mid or low ponytail, then secure it with an elastic.

Step 2: Divide the ponytail into three equal sections.

Step 3: Braid the ponytail all the way down in a simple three-strand braid.

Step 4: Secure the end of the braid with a small clear elastic.

Step 5: Gently pull at the braid loops to make the braid look fuller and softer.

Step 6: Finish with hair spray and add a ribbon or decorative clip if desired.

SIMPLE BRAIDED PONYTAIL
6-STEP GUIDE

STEP 1

Brush your hair smoothly and gather it into a mid or low ponytail, then secure it with an elastic.

STEP 2

Divide the ponytail into three equal sections.

STEP 3

Braid the ponytail all the way down in a simple three-strand braid.

STEP 4

Secure the end of the braid with a small clear elastic.

STEP 5

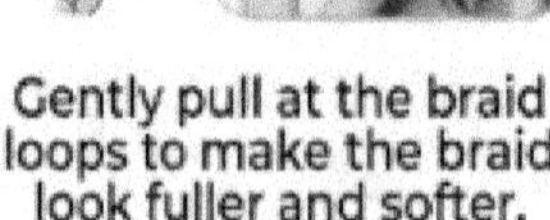

Gently pull at the braid loops to make the braid look fuller and softer.

STEP 6

Finish with hair spray and add a ribbon or decorative clip if desired.

Common Mistakes

- Braid looks too thin
- Sections feel uneven
- Ponytail base looks messy
- Braid starts loosening at the end

Quick Fixes

- Pull the braid gently wider after securing it
- Divide the hair evenly before braiding
- Smooth the ponytail before starting the braid
- Use a tight small elastic at the braid end

Make It Your Own

- Wrap a strand of hair around the main elastic
- Add pearls or mini flowers along the braid
- Pull out soft front strands for a softer finish

Heads-Up

This hairstyle is simple, but neat sectioning makes all the difference. If your layers are short, use a bit of spray before braiding to keep the ends from slipping out.

The simple braided ponytail is proof that even the easiest styles can still look wedding-ready.

30. Twisted Side Bun

Best for: Medium to long hair

Hair type: Straight, wavy, lightly curly

Skill level: Beginner to intermediate

Time needed: 10–15 minutes

Best for: Bridesmaids, wedding guests, romantic weddings, evening receptions

Works with: Pearl pins, floral clips, jeweled combs, soft curls

Hold level: Medium to strong

The twisted side bun is a soft and elegant hairstyle that feels romantic from every angle. Placed slightly to one side, it gives the look a graceful and feminine touch that works beautifully for weddings and formal events. It is a lovely choice when you want an updo that feels polished but not too strict.

You'll Need

- Hairbrush or comb
- Hair elastic
- Bobby pins
- Hair spray
- Optional: curling iron, decorative comb, pearl pins

Before You Start

This hairstyle looks best on dry hair with a little texture. If you want a softer finish, add loose curls first. Side buns work especially well when the hair has some natural grip, so use dry shampoo or texture spray if needed.

Step-by-Step

Step 1: Brush your hair gently and part it as desired, then gather it low to one side near the nape.

Step 2: Secure the hair into a low side ponytail with an elastic.

Step 3: Twist the ponytail loosely and wrap it around the base to form a side bun.

Step 4: Pin the bun securely with bobby pins, shaping it as you go.

Step 5: Loosen a few strands near the face and crown to create a softer romantic effect.

Step 6: Finish with hair spray and add decorative pins or a comb if desired.

TWISTED SIDE BUN
6-STEP GUIDE

STEP 1

Brush your hair gently and part it as desired, then gather it low to one side near the nape.

STEP 2

Secure the hair into a low side ponytail with an elastic.

STEP 3

Twist the ponytail loosely and wrap it around the base to form a side bun.

STEP 4

Pin the bun securely with bobby pins, shaping it as you go.

STEP 5

Loosen a few strands near the face and crown to create a softer romantic effect.

STEP 6

Finish with hair spray and add decorative pins or a comb if desired.

Common Mistakes
- Bun feels off-balance
- Side placement looks too low or too far back
- Pins show too much
- Front looks too flat

Quick Fixes
- Check the bun from the front and side before final pinning
- Position the bun just behind the ear area for the best shape
- Hide visible pins beneath the bun folds
- Gently lift the crown with your fingers for softness

Make It Your Own
- Add curls before styling for extra volume
- Place pearl pins on one side of the bun
- Leave face-framing strands loose for a romantic finish

Heads-Up

Because this bun sits to one side, placement matters more than with a center low bun. Practice once first to find the most flattering side and height for your face shape.

The twisted side bun brings together softness, elegance, and just enough detail to feel truly special.

Theme-Based Wedding Hairstyles

Your wedding hairstyle should do more than look beautiful on its own. It should feel like a natural part of your full bridal look. The right hairstyle brings together your dress, accessories, makeup, venue, and the overall mood of the day. A soft braided crown may feel perfect for a garden wedding, while a sleek low bun may suit a modern or formal celebration much better. When your hairstyle matches the theme, everything feels more polished, balanced, and intentional.

Choosing a hairstyle by theme also makes decision-making easier. Instead of getting overwhelmed by too many options, you can focus on styles that truly fit your wedding setting and personal style. Whether your wedding is classic, romantic, boho, beachy, rustic, or glamorous, there are certain hairstyle shapes, finishes, and accessories that work better than others. This section will help you understand those matches so you can choose a look that feels beautiful, practical, and true to you.

How to Choose the Right Theme-Based Wedding Hairstyle

- Start with your **wedding vibe**. Ask yourself if your wedding feels classic, romantic, modern, boho, rustic, beachy, glamorous, or minimal.
- Look at your **dress style**. A heavily detailed gown may pair better with a simpler hairstyle, while a clean dress can handle a more detailed hair look.
- Think about your **venue**. Indoor ballroom weddings, outdoor garden weddings, beach weddings, and destination weddings all need different hairstyle choices.
- Consider the **weather**. Humidity, wind, heat, and even light rain can affect how well a hairstyle holds.
- Be honest about your **hair type and length**. Some styles look amazing in photos but may not work as well on very fine, thick, short, or highly layered hair.
- Match the hairstyle to your **comfort level**. If you want a relaxed and natural look, do not force a very stiff or formal hairstyle.

- Think about your **accessories** early. Veils, tiaras, floral pins, combs, and statement clips can change which hairstyles work best.
- Choose a style that fits your **face shape and features**, but do not overthink it. The goal is balance, softness, and confidence.
- Decide whether the style needs to last through just the ceremony or the **full day**, including photos, dancing, and travel.
- Always do at least one **trial run** before the wedding so you can see how the hairstyle looks, feels, and lasts.

Quick Tips Before You Decide

- Pick a hairstyle that feels like **you**, not just one that is trending.
- Save 3 to 5 reference styles that match your theme before making a final choice.
- Avoid choosing a hairstyle only because it looks good on someone with a very different hair type.
- If your dress has a standout neckline or back design, choose a hairstyle that helps show it off.
- For outdoor weddings, favour styles with **better hold** and less risk of falling flat.
- For soft and romantic themes, loose texture and gentle face-framing pieces usually work well.
- For modern and formal themes, clean lines and smooth finishes often look stronger.
- If you are wearing a veil, test the hairstyle with the veil during your trial.
- Keep a **backup style option** in mind in case weather or timing changes your plan.
- The best hairstyle is one that looks beautiful AND feels secure for the whole event.
- **A wedding hairstyle should not fight the theme-it should complete it.**

31. Boho Floral Braid

Best for: Medium to long hair

    Hair type: Wavy, straight, lightly curly

    Skill level: Beginner to intermediate

    Time needed: 10–15 minutes

    Best for: Outdoor weddings, garden weddings, boho themes

    Works with: Fresh flowers, floral pins, baby's breath, soft veil

    Hold level: Medium

The boho floral braid is a soft, dreamy hairstyle that feels natural, romantic, and full of charm. With its slightly loose texture and delicate floral touches, it is perfect for brides who want an effortless look that still feels special. This hairstyle works beautifully for outdoor celebrations and pairs especially well with lace, flowy fabrics, and relaxed bridal styling.

    You'll Need

- Hairbrush or comb
- Hair elastic
- Bobby pins
- Hair spray
- Optional: curling iron, texture spray, small flowers or floral pins

Before You Start

This style looks best with a little texture, so slightly waved or second-day hair works very well. If your hair is too soft, use a texture spray before braiding to help the braid hold its shape and appear fuller.

Step-by-Step

Step 1: Brush your hair gently and create a soft center or side part, depending on your preference.

Step 2: Gather your hair over one shoulder and begin a loose three-strand braid starting near the side of your head or from the back.

Step 3: Continue braiding down the length of your hair, keeping the braid relaxed rather than tight.

Step 4: Secure the end with a small elastic and gently pull at the braid sections to make it look fuller and softer.

Step 5: Tuck in small flowers or floral pins along the braid, spacing them evenly for a natural finish.

Step 6: Set everything with hair spray and adjust a few face-framing strands for a soft boho effect.

BOHO FLORAL BRAID
6-STEP GUIDE

STEP
1

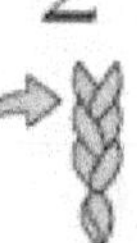

Brush your hair gently
and create a soft center
side part, depending on
your preference.

STEP
2

Gather your hair over one
shoulder and begin a loose
three-strand braid starting
near the side of your head
or from the back.

STEP
3

Continue braiding down
the length of your hair,
keeping the braid relaxed
rather than tight.

STEP
4

Secure the end with a small
elastic and gently pull at the
braid sections to make it
look fuller and softer.

STEP
5

Tuck in small flowers or
floral pins along the braid,
spacing them evenly for a
natural finish.

STEP
6

Set everything with hair
spray and adjust a few
face-framing strands for a
soft boho effect.

Common Mistakes
- Braid looks too tight and stiff
- Flowers feel heavy or uneven
- Braid looks thin
- Hair slips out around the crown

Quick Fixes
- Gently pull apart the braid to soften the look
- Use lightweight floral pins instead of large flowers
- Add texture spray before braiding for more fullness
- Secure loose crown pieces with hidden bobby pins

Make It Your Own
- Add baby's breath for a delicate bridal touch
- Pull out soft face-framing pieces for a more relaxed look
- Use a side braid for a more romantic finish

Heads-Up

This hairstyle is meant to look soft and slightly undone, so do not worry if it is not perfectly neat. Brides with very silky hair may need extra texture spray and a few hidden pins to keep the braid secure.

The boho floral braid is soft, feminine, and effortlessly beautiful.

32. Beachy Bridal Waves

Best for: Medium to long hair

    Hair type: Straight, wavy, lightly curly

    Skill level: Beginner

    Time needed: 10–15 minutes

    Best for: Beach weddings, destination weddings, summer ceremonies

    Works with: Floral clips, side pins, minimal veil, pearl accessories

    Hold level: Light to medium

Beachy bridal waves are perfect for brides who want a soft, fresh, and relaxed style without losing elegance. This hairstyle creates movement and texture while still looking polished enough for a wedding day. It is especially beautiful for beach or outdoor ceremonies where a more natural and breezier bridal look feels just right.

    You'll Need

- Hairbrush or wide-tooth comb
- Curling iron or wand
- Heat protectant
- Hair spray
- Optional: sea salt spray, floral clip, shine spray

Before You Start

Apply heat protectant before curling. This style works best when the waves are not too tight, so aim for loose bends and soft texture rather than perfect curls. A bit of sea salt spray can help add that beachy finish.

Step-by-Step

Step 1: Brush your hair and apply heat protectant evenly from mid-length to ends.

Step 2: Curl large sections of hair away from your face using a curling wand or iron, leaving the ends slightly straighter.

Step 3: Let the curls cool fully before touching them so they hold better.

Step 4: Gently run your fingers or a wide-tooth comb through the curls to soften them into loose waves.

Step 5: Add a little sea salt spray or light texture spray to enhance movement, then place a floral clip or decorative pin if desired.

Step 6: Finish with a light mist of hair spray to hold the waves without making them stiff.

BEACHY BRIDAL WAVES
6-STEP GUIDE

Brush your hair and apply
heat protectant evenly
from mid-length to ends.

Curl large sections of hair
away from your face using a
curling wand or iron, leaving
the ends slightly straighter.

Let the curls cool fully
before touching them so
they hold better.

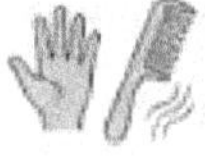

Gently run your fingers or a
wide-tooth comb through
the curls to soften them
into loose waves.

Add a little sea salt spray or
light texture spray to enhance
movement, then place a floral
clip or decorative pin if desired.

Finish with a light mist of
hair spray to hold the waves
without making them stiff.

Common Mistakes

- Waves look too tight and formal
- Hair falls flat quickly
- Ends look frizzy
- Waves lose shape in humidity

Quick Fixes

- Brush through curls more to loosen them
- Let each curl cool before combing it out
- Add a little smoothing serum to the ends
- Use a flexible hold spray for better lasting power

Make It Your Own

- Add a side clip for a soft bridal accent
- Tuck one side behind the ear for a relaxed beach look
- Pair with tiny pearl pins for a more elegant finish

Heads-Up

This style looks best when it feels soft and natural, not overdone. Brides with very straight or heavy hair may need extra spray or smaller curl sections to help the waves last longer.

Beachy bridal waves bring together softness, movement, and effortless bridal charm.

33. Vintage Hollywood Waves

Best for: Medium to long hair

    Hair type: Straight, wavy

    Skill level: Intermediate

    Time needed: 15 minutes

    Best for: Glam weddings, evening receptions, vintage themes

    Works with: Side combs, crystal clips, elegant veil, bold earrings

    Hold level: Strong

Vintage Hollywood waves are all about timeless glamour. Smooth, sculpted, and polished, this hairstyle creates a dramatic side-swept look that feels elegant and luxurious. It is ideal for brides who love old-Hollywood beauty and want a hairstyle that looks refined, classic, and unforgettable in photos.

    You'll Need

- Hairbrush or comb

- Curling iron
- Sectioning clips
- Hair spray
- Optional: shine spray, decorative side comb, smoothing serum

Before You Start

This style works best on smooth hair with a deep side part. The key is to keep the waves uniform and polished, so take care when curling and shaping each section.

Step-by-Step

Step 1: Brush your hair smooth and create a deep side part for that classic Hollywood shape.

Step 2: Curl medium sections of hair in the same direction, keeping the curls even throughout.

Step 3: Let the curls cool completely, then gently brush them out with a soft brush to form smooth waves.

Step 4: Use your hands or clips to shape the waves neatly, especially around the front and sides.

Step 5: Add a little shine spray or smoothing serum, and place a decorative comb on the fuller side if desired.

Step 6: Finish with a firm hold hair spray to keep the waves sleek and defined.

VINTAGE HOLLYWOOD WAVES
6-STEP GUIDE

STEP 1

Brush your hair smooth and create a deep side part for that classic Hollywood shape.

STEP 2

Curl medium sections of hair in the same direction, keeping the curls even throughout.

STEP 3

Let the curls cool completely, then gently brush them out with a soft brush to form smooth waves.

STEP 4

Use your hands or clips to shape the waves neatly, especially around the front and sides.

STEP 5

Add a little shine spray or smoothing serum, and place a decorative comb on the fuller side if desired.

STEP 6

Finish with a firm hold hair spray to keep the waves sleek and defined.

Common Mistakes

- Waves look messy instead of sculpted
- Curls go in different directions
- Hair becomes frizzy when brushed
- Front section falls flat

Quick Fixes

- Curl all sections in the same direction
- Brush gently and slowly to blend the curls
- Use smoothing serum lightly before final shaping
- Clip the front wave for a few minutes to help it set

Make It Your Own

- Add a crystal clip above one ear
- Pair with bold earrings for extra glam
- Keep one side tucked back for a more dramatic bridal finish

Heads-Up

This hairstyle looks stunning, but it usually takes one or two practice runs to get the shaping right. Brides with layered hair may need extra spray and clips to keep the front waves smooth and defined.

Vintage Hollywood waves are graceful, polished, and full of old-world bridal glamour.

34. Glam High Bun

Best for: Medium to long hair

Hair type: Straight, wavy

Skill level: Intermediate

Time needed: 10–15 minutes

Best for: Glam weddings, formal ceremonies, evening receptions

Works with: Tiara, crystal pins, veil, statement earrings

Hold level: Strong

The glam high bun is sleek, lifted, and instantly elegant. This hairstyle creates a clean and refined silhouette while drawing attention to the face, neckline, and dress details. It is a favorite for brides who want a polished, confident look with a modern and luxurious feel.

You'll Need

• Hairbrush or comb

- Hair elastic
- Bobby pins
- Hair spray
- Optional: bun donut, smoothing serum, crystal pins, tiara

Before You Start

For the best finish, start with smooth, dry hair. If your hair is frizzy or textured, use a little smoothing serum before styling. A bun donut can help create extra fullness and shape if you want a more dramatic result.

Step-by-Step

Step 1: Brush your hair upward and gather it into a high ponytail at the crown of your head.

Step 2: Secure the ponytail tightly with an elastic and smooth down any bumps or flyaway.

Step 3: Twist the ponytail around its base, or wrap it over a bun donut if using one, to create a full bun shape.

Step 4: Secure the bun with bobby pins, making sure the shape feels balanced and firm.

Step 5: Smooth the front and sides with a little serum or spray, then add crystal pins or a tiara if desired.

Step 6: Finish with a strong hold hair spray to lock the style in place.

GLAM HIGH BUN
6-STEP GUIDE

Brush your hair upward and gather it into a high ponytail at the crown of your head.

Secure the ponytail tightly with an elastic and smooth down any bumps or flyaways.

Twist the ponytail around its base, or wrap it over a bun donut if using one, to create a full bun shape.

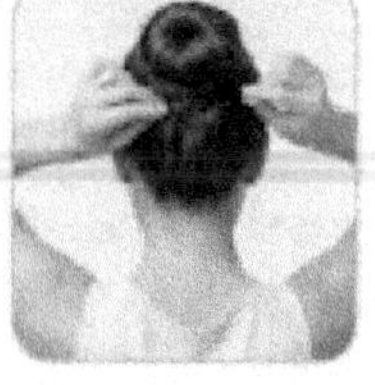

Secure the bun with bobby pins, making sure the shape feels balanced and firm.

Smooth the front and sides with a little serum or spray, then add crystal pins or a tiara if desired.

Finish with a strong hold hair spray to lock the style in place.

Common Mistakes

- Bun feels too small or flat
- Hair has bumps near the crown
- Flyaway make the style look messy
- Bun shifts out of place

Quick Fixes

- Use a bun donut for more fullness
- Smooth sections carefully before tying the ponytail
- Apply a little serum for a sleek finish
- Add extra pins around the base for stronger hold

Make It Your Own

- Add crystal pins for a glamorous bridal touch
- Wrap a small strand of hair around the bun base for a polished finish
- Pair with a tiara or dramatic veil for extra elegance

Heads-Up

This style is best for brides who want a clean, formal look that lasts well through the day. Brides with very layered hair may need additional pins and spray to keep the bun looking sleek.

The glam high bun is bold, refined, and effortlessly bridal.

35. Rustic Loose Side Braid

Best for: Medium to long hair

    Hair type: Wavy, straight, lightly curly

    Skill level: Beginner

    Time needed: 10–15 minutes

    Best for: Rustic weddings, barn weddings, garden ceremonies

    Works with: Floral pins, ribbon, soft veil, dried flowers

    Hold level: Medium

The rustic loose side braid is a charming hairstyle that feels soft, natural, and warm. It has an easy beauty that suits outdoor weddings perfectly, especially when paired with textured dresses, natural flowers, and relaxed styling. This look is ideal for brides who want something pretty and practical without feeling too formal.

    You'll Need

- Hairbrush or comb
- Hair elastic
- Bobby pins
- Hair spray
- Optional: texture spray, ribbon, floral pins, dried flowers

Before You Start

This hairstyle looks best with a little volume and texture. If your hair is very smooth, use texture spray first to help the braid stay fuller and prevent it from slipping apart.

Step-by-Step

Step 1: Brush your hair and create a soft part, then sweep all of your hair over one shoulder.

Step 2: Begin a loose three-strand braid, keeping the tension soft so the style stays relaxed.

Step 3: Continue braiding to the ends and secure it with a small elastic.

Step 4: Gently pull at the braid sections to make the braid fuller and more textured.

Step 5: Add floral pins, ribbon, or small dried flowers along the braid for a rustic bridal touch.

Step 6: Set the style with hair spray and loosen a few face-framing strands for softness.

RUSTIC LOOSE SIDE BRAID
6-STEP GUIDE

STEP 1

Brush your hair and create a soft part, then sweep all of your hair over one shoulder.

STEP 2

Begin a loose three-strand braid, keeping the tension soft so the style stays relaxed.

STEP 3

Continue braiding to the ends and secure it with a small elastic.

STEP 4

Gently pull at the braid sections to make the braid fuller and more textured.

STEP 5

Add floral pins, ribbon, or small dried flowers along the braid for a rustic bridal touch.

STEP 6

Set the style with hair spray and loosen a few face-framing strands for softness.

Common Mistakes
- Braid looks too tight and plain
- Hair falls out near the front
- Braid looks thin
- Accessories feel uneven

Quick Fixes
- Pull apart the braid gently for a softer shape
- Secure front pieces with hidden bobby pins
- Add texture spray before braiding for fullness
- Place accessories lightly and space them evenly

Make It Your Own
- Add ribbon woven into the braid for a rustic detail
- Use dried flowers for a soft countryside look
- Leave gentle waves around the face for a romantic finish

Heads-Up

This style is very beginner-friendly, but it still benefits from a quick practice run. Brides with very fine hair may want to curl the hair lightly first so the braid looks fuller and holds better.

The rustic loose side braid is simple, pretty, and full of relaxed bridal charm.

Accessories That Work

The right hair accessory can make a simple hairstyle look elegant, polished, and bridal. But not every accessory works with every style. The best accessories add beauty without feeling heavy, distracting, or hard to secure.

The key is simple: **choose your hairstyle first, then choose the accessory**. A sleek low bun needs something different from loose curls or a braided crown. Your accessory should match the hairstyle, your dress, your wedding style, and how long you need the look to last.

Start with the hairstyle first

One common mistake bride make is choosing an accessory before choosing the hairstyle. A beautiful veil, tiara, or floral clip may catch your eye, but it may not suit the final hairstyle you choose.

Pick your hairstyle first, then choose an accessory that fits:

- the shape of the hairstyle
- the volume of the hair
- the formality of the wedding
- whether you are wearing a veil
- how secure the style needs to be?

The hairstyle leads. The accessory supports.

Best bridal accessories to consider

Veils

Veils are timeless and romantic. They work especially well with low buns, chignons, French twists, half-up styles, and soft curls with pinned sections.

Tips:

- test placement during your trial run
- secure with strong pins or a comb
- make sure it does not hide important hairstyle details
- avoid discomfort or pulling

Hair combs

Hair combs add shine and detail without taking over the whole look. They work well with side-swept styles, low buns, half-up hairstyles, and vintage-inspired looks.

Choose a comb that fits the size of your hairstyle. Too large can feel heavy. Too small may disappear.

Hairpins

Hairpins are flexible and easy to use. They work beautifully in buns, twists, braids, pinned curls, and soft updos. Pearl pins, crystal pins, and floral pins are especially popular for bridal looks.

Use them when you want:

- soft detail
- flexible placement
- light accents
- easy styling adjustments

Tiaras and headbands

Tiaras and bridal headbands create a more formal, classic look. They work best with sleek buns, polished half-up styles, soft glam curls, and classic updos.

If you choose a bold tiara or headband, keep the rest of the accessories simple. One statement piece is enough.

Floral accessories

Fresh flowers and floral clips feel soft, romantic, and natural. They are perfect for garden, beach, boho, and outdoor weddings, especially with braided crowns, textured buns, and loose updos.

Use flowers carefully:

- test them before the wedding
- avoid overfilling the hairstyle
- match them with the bouquet or wedding theme

Clips and barrettes

Clips and barrettes are stylish, simple, and easy to wear. They are great for modern or minimal bridal looks, especially with side parts, short hair, half-up styles, sleek buns, and pinned curls.

A small pearl or crystal clip can finish the hairstyle beautifully without too much effort.

Match the accessory to the hairstyle

- **Buns and chignons:** veil, comb, pearl pins, floral accents
- **Loose curls:** side clip, light comb, floral pin, delicate vine
- **Braided styles:** small pins, mini flowers, pearl details
- **Half-up hairstyles:** comb, clip, veil, vine, small pins
- **Short hair:** headband, side comb, clip, mini floral piece

Choose accessories that add to the hairstyle, not fight with it.

Match the accessory to the wedding style

- **Classic wedding:** pearls, sleek veils, elegant combs
- **Romantic wedding:** floral pieces, delicate vines, soft sparkle
- **Boho wedding:** flowers, leafy vines, textured accents
- **Glam wedding:** crystals, bold combs, refined tiaras
- **Minimal modern wedding:** one clean barrette, polished comb, or simple veil

Everything should feel like part of the same bridal story.

Comfort matters

A beautiful accessory can become uncomfortable very quickly if it is too heavy, sharp, or hard to secure. Before choosing one, ask:

- is it too heavy?
- does it pull on the scalp?
- will it stay in place?
- does it feel comfortable for hours?

Comfort is part of confidence.

Avoid over-accessorizing

Too many accessories can make the hairstyle feel busy and cluttered.
A good rule:

- if the hairstyle is detailed, keep the accessory simple
- if the hairstyle is simple, the accessory can stand out more
- if one piece is bold, let it be the focus

Balance always looks better than excess.

Test everything before the wedding

Never wait until the wedding day to test your accessories. Try them during your hair trial, take photos from all angles, and wear them long enough to check comfort and hold.
Check:

- does it stay secure?

- does it look good in photos?
- does it work with your veil and earrings?
- does it still feel comfortable after some time?

The best accessory is not the biggest or most expensive. It is the one that fits your hairstyle, supports your bridal look, feels comfortable, and stays beautiful throughout the day.

When chosen well, accessories do more than decorate the hair. They help complete the bridal look. **That is what works.**

Shop Our Recommended Accessories

To make your bridal hairstyling journey easier, you can explore our recommended hair accessories and styling essentials on the website. From elegant pins and combs to bridal-friendly tools and finishing touches, these handpicked picks can help you create a look that feels beautiful, secure, and wedding-ready.

Visit **MyBrideHairs.com/products** to explore the collection.

Hairstyles by Face Shape

Your wedding hairstyle should do more than look pretty. It should also help **balance your features**, highlight what you love most about your face, and make you feel confident from every angle.

Face shape is one useful guide when choosing a hairstyle. The right style can add softness, create height, balance width, or draw attention to your eyes, cheekbones, or smile. That said, face shape is only one part of the decision. Your hair type, dress neckline, veil, accessories, and personal style matter too.

Use this section as a guide, not a rulebook. The best hairstyle is always the one that makes you feel the most beautiful on your big day. **Confidence is the final touch.**

How to Determine Your Face Shape

Before choosing a hairstyle, take a quick look at your face in the mirror with your hair pulled back.

Pay attention to:

- the width of your forehead
- the width of your cheekbones
- the width of your jawline
- the overall length of your face
- whether your chin is soft, pointed, or angular

Most faces fall into one of these common shapes:

- round
- square
- heart
- oval
- long or oblong

Do not worry if your face seems to fit more than one type. Many women have a mix of features. In that case, choose the hairstyle advice that feels most flattering to you. **Use the mirror, not strict labels.**

Hairstyles for Round Faces

Round faces usually have soft curves with similar width and length. The goal is often to create a little more **length and definition.**

What works best

Hairstyles that add height at the crown can help elongate the face. Side parts are also flattering because they break up facial symmetry and create a more sculpted look. Soft waves that fall below the chin can make the face appear longer and slimmer.

Great options include:

- top knots with soft volume
- low buns with height at the crown
- side-swept curls
- long, loose waves
- half-up styles with crown lift
- soft side braids

What to avoid

Avoid styles that add too much width at the cheeks. Very round buns, heavy volume at the sides, and blunt chin-length cuts can make the face appear wider.

Best styling tips

- tease the crown slightly for height
- choose a side part instead of a center part
- leave a few face-framing pieces to add softness
- keep volume higher, not wider

Best accessories

- side combs
- delicate hair vines
- vertical accessories that draw the eye upward

For round faces, think HEIGHT over WIDTH.

Hairstyles for Square Faces

Square faces often have a broad forehead and a strong jawline. The goal is to **soften angles** and add movement around the face.

What works best

Soft curls, waves, and layered styles can help balance a square face beautifully. Loose updos and side-parted styles work especially well because they reduce harsh lines and create a more romantic look.

Great options include:

- loose chignons
- soft low buns
- side-swept waves
- romantic half-up hairstyles
- textured braids
- styles with long, soft bangs

What to avoid

Avoid overly sleek, flat, or sharp-edged styles if you want a softer look. Tight pulled-back hair with no movement can make the jawline appear stronger.

Best styling tips

- add curls or waves around the face
- leave soft strands near the jawline
- avoid making the crown too flat
- choose rounded shapes instead of stiff shapes

Best accessories

- floral pins
- soft pearl combs
- curved or delicate pieces instead of very sharp geometric designs

For square faces, think SOFTNESS and MOVEMENT.

Hairstyles for Heart-Shaped Faces

Heart-shaped faces are usually wider at the forehead and narrower at the chin. The goal is to **balance the upper face** and add a little fullness around the lower half.

What works best

Styles that bring attention lower on the face are often most flattering. Chin-length or longer styles, soft waves, and side parts can help create balance. Wispy bangs or side-swept fringe can also soften a broader forehead.

Great options include:

- side-swept curls
- low buns
- soft waves starting below the cheekbones
- half-up hairstyles with loose ends
- styles with chin-level fullness
- gentle side braids

What to avoid

Avoid very full volume at the crown combined with very tight sides, as that can make the forehead appear even wider. Very short, puffy styles may also throw off balance.

Best styling tips

- keep the crown soft, not too high
- add fullness near the jawline or shoulders
- try side-swept bangs or wispy front pieces
- keep the look light and romantic

Best accessories

- side clips
- low-placed flowers
- accessories placed near the side or back rather than directly on top

For heart-shaped faces, think BALANCE from forehead to chin.

Hairstyles for Oval Faces

Oval faces are often considered the most versatile because the proportions are naturally balanced. This means many hairstyles work beautifully.

What works best

Almost any style can suit an oval face, including buns, braids, waves, sleek looks, and half-up styles. The key is to choose based on your hair type, dress style, and the feature you want to highlight.

Great options include:

- sleek buns
- classic chignons
- loose romantic waves
- braided crowns
- half-up curls
- polished ponytail styles

What to watch for

Because oval faces are so balanced, your hairstyle choice should focus more on your overall bridal look rather than trying to correct proportions.

Best styling tips

- use bangs to draw attention to the eyes
- use pulled-back styles to highlight cheekbones
- match the hairstyle to your dress neckline and wedding vibe
- choose structure or softness based on your personal style

Best accessories

- almost anything works well
- veils, tiaras, vines, combs, pearls, and flowers can all suit an oval face

For oval faces, think FREEDOM and FEATURE HIGHLIGHTING.

Hairstyles for Long or Oblong Faces

Long or oblong faces are more vertical in shape, so the goal is often to create a little more **width and balance** while avoiding extra height.

What works best

Styles with side volume can help a long face look more balanced. Waves, curls, and fuller styles around the cheeks or jawline often work very well. Bangs can also help visually shorten the face.

Great options include:

- soft shoulder-length waves
- low buns with width
- side curls
- half-up styles with side fullness
- braided styles with texture at the sides
- curtain bangs or soft fringe

What to avoid

Avoid too much height at the crown, very tight top knots, or styles that pull everything straight back with no softness.

Best styling tips

- add width at the sides
- keep volume low or mid-level, not too high
- consider bangs or face-framing layers
- use texture to create a fuller look

Best accessories

- side accessories
- medium-width combs
- floral accents placed slightly off-center

For long faces, think WIDTH and BALANCE.

Quick Face Shape Matching Guide

Use this cheat sheet when you need a fast answer:

Face Shape	Main Goal	Best Style Features	Avoid
Round	Add length	Height at crown, side part, long waves	Width at cheeks
Square	Soften angles	Waves, curls, loose updos, side parts	Very flat or severe styles
Heart	Balance forehead and chin	Side fringe, low buns, chin-level fullness	Too much crown volume
Oval	Highlight best features	Almost any style	Nothing major-focus on overall look
Long/ Oblong	Add width	Side volume, waves, fringe	Too much height

Face Shape Is a Guide, Not a Rule

Your face shape can help you narrow down your options, but it should never make you feel limited. A hairstyle may look amazing on you because of your texture, your confidence, your smile, or the way it matches your dress and accessories.

The most flattering hairstyle is the one you wear with confidence.

Quick Fixes and Troubleshooting

Even the most beautiful wedding hairstyle can run into small problems. A few loose pins, a little humidity, or flat volume can change the look quickly. The good news is that most hairstyle issues can be fixed in just a few minutes with the right tools and a calm approach.

This section will help you solve the most common bridal hair problems so your hairstyle stays beautiful, secure, and photo-ready throughout the day.

Stay calm. Small fixes can make a BIG difference.

1. Frizz and Flyaway

Frizz and flyaway are one of the most common bridal hair issues, especially in humid weather or after moving around a lot.

Why it happens

- humidity in the air
- dry or damaged hair
- too much brushing after styling
- not enough smoothing product
- hair rubbing against clothing or hands

Quick fix

- spray a little hairspray onto your hands or a soft brush, then gently smooth the surface of the hair
- use a small amount of anti-frizz serum only on the top layer
- smooth stubborn flyaway with a clean toothbrush or edge brush
- avoid adding too much product, or the hair may look greasy

Prevention tip

Prep the hair with a smoothing serum or anti-frizz cream before styling, especially for outdoor weddings.

Smooth, don't soak. Less product gives a cleaner finish.

2. Curls Falling Flat

Soft curls and waves can lose their shape if the hair is too heavy, too clean, or not set properly.

Why it happens

- hair is freshly washed and too soft
- curls were too large or loose
- not enough holding product
- curls were touched before cooling
- weather or sweat softened the style

Quick fix

- re-curl only the loose sections instead of the whole hairstyle
- let each curl cool completely before touching it
- mist lightly with hairspray and pin the curl up for a few minutes to set it again
- scrunch gently to bring back bounce

Prevention tip

Use a light mousse or texture spray before curling, and let curls cool fully before brushing or styling them.

Cool curls hold better. Heat shapes them, but cooling locks them in.

3. Bun or Updo Feels Loose

A bun or updo can start to loosen after walking, dancing, hugging, or adjusting the veil.

Why it happens

- not enough pins
- pins were inserted in the wrong direction
- hair was too silky or slippery
- bun was too heavy for the pin support
- hair was not anchored properly at the base

Quick fix

- add a few more bobby pins where the hairstyle feels loose

- cross two pins in an X shape for a stronger hold
- spray a little hairspray on the pins before inserting them
- tighten the loose section gently before pinning again
- if needed, remove one small part and rebuild just that area

Prevention tip

Create a secure ponytail or anchor point first before building the bun or updo around it.

A strong base creates a strong hairstyle.

4. Crown Looks Flat

A flat crown can make the hairstyle feel less bridal and less polished, especially in photos.

Why it happens

- not enough lift at the roots
- heavy hair pulling downward
- no teasing or root support
- top section smoothed too tightly

Quick fix

- gently lift the top section with a tail comb
- tease lightly underneath the crown area
- smooth the outer layer softly over the teased section
- add a little root-lifting spray or dry shampoo for grip

Prevention tip

Build a little volume before the final hairstyle is secured, not after everything is pinned.

Soft volume adds elegance without making the style look stiff.

5. Braid Looks Thin or Uneven

Braids can sometimes look too flat, too small, or uneven from side to side.

Why it happens

- hair sections were not equal
- hair was too smooth and slipped during braiding
- braid was pulled too tight in some places and too loose in others
- not enough texture in the hair

Quick fix

- gently pull the edges of the braid outward a little to make it look fuller
- redo only the messy section if needed
- use texture spray before braiding
- check section sizes in a mirror before continuing

Prevention tip

Braids usually look better on hair with some texture rather than very soft, silky hair.

A slightly imperfect braid can still look romantic, but it should feel balanced.

6. Pins Showing Too Much

Visible pins can take away from the softness and beauty of the hairstyle.

Why it happens

- pins were placed on the outer surface
- hair was too thin over the pinned area
- pin color did not match hair color
- hairstyle shifted after pinning

Quick fix

- slide visible pins deeper into the hairstyle
- cover the area with a small twisted strand or accessory
- replace bright pins with pins closer to the hair color

- add one decorative pin over the area if needed

Prevention tip

Always keep a mix of blonde, brown, and black pins ready if you are unsure which blends best.

Hidden support makes the hairstyle look cleaner and more professional.

7. Hairstyle Feels Too Tight

A bridal hairstyle should feel secure, but not painful.

Why it happens

- elastics are tied too tightly
- pins are pressing against the scalp
- sections were pulled too hard
- too much teasing created scalp tension

Quick fix

- remove and reset the painful pin
- gently loosen the tight section with your fingers
- if needed, take out one or two hidden pins without changing the whole style
- soften face-framing pieces slightly to reduce tension

Prevention tip

Check comfort during the trial run. If it hurts during practice, it will feel worse on the wedding day.

A beautiful hairstyle should still feel wearable for hours.

8. Veil Slipping or Not Staying in Place

A veil can shift if it is not anchored properly into the hairstyle.

Why it happens

- veil comb was not inserted into a stable section
- hairstyle was too soft where the veil was placed
- veil was too heavy for the hairstyle structure

- not enough hidden support pins

Quick fix

- place the veil comb into a secure bun, twist, or teased section
- use bobby pins around the comb to lock it in place
- cross pins over the veil comb for extra hold
- check the balance so it does not pull on one side

Prevention tip

Always test the veil with the hairstyle during a trial run, not on the wedding day for the first time.

The veil should sit securely without pulling the style apart.

9. Accessory Keeps Falling Out

Hair vines, flowers, pearls, and clips need support, not just decoration.

Why it happens

- accessory is too heavy
- accessory was placed on a weak section
- not enough pins were used to secure it
- hair is too soft or slippery

Quick fix

- move the accessory to a more secure part of the hairstyle
- pin it from both sides
- use smaller hidden pins underneath the decoration
- add texture spray before placing it again

Prevention tip

Lightweight accessories are usually easier and safer for long wear.

Pretty is good. Secure is better.

10. Hair Looks Greasy After Styling

Too much serum, spray, or oil can make the hairstyle lose freshness.

Why it happens

- too much product used at once
- serum applied near the roots
- product layered too many times
- hair was already oily before styling

Quick fix

- dab gently with a tissue to remove excess shine
- use a small amount of dry shampoo at the roots
- avoid adding more serum
- if only one area looks greasy, try covering it with a twist, braid, or accessory

Prevention tip

Use styling products in small amounts and build slowly only if needed.

It is easier to add more product than to remove too much.

11. Hair Becomes Messy in Wind or Humidity

Outdoor weddings can be beautiful, but weather can affect the hairstyle quickly.

Why it happens

- high humidity
- strong wind
- not enough hold
- style was too soft for outdoor conditions

Quick fix

- smooth the outer layer with hands and hairspray
- pin back loose strands neatly
- tighten any loose twist or bun
- use decorative pins to hide quick repairs

Prevention tip

Choose stronger styles like buns, twists, braided updos, or pinned half-up looks for outdoor weddings.

Match the hairstyle to the weather, not just the mood board.

12. Style Looks Different on One Side

Sometimes one side may appear fuller, tighter, or higher than the other.

Why it happens

- uneven sectioning
- one side pinned more tightly
- curls brushed differently
- no final mirror checks from all angles

Quick fix

- step back and check the hairstyle from front, side, and back
- loosen one side gently if it looks too tight
- add one or two pins to balance the weaker side
- pull out a few soft strands to make both sides look more even

Prevention tip

Take photos during your trial run. Small balance issues show up more clearly in pictures than in a mirror.

The camera catches what the mirror may miss.

13. What to Do If You Are Running Out of Time

Sometimes the hairstyle does not go as planned, and time becomes the biggest problem.

Quick fix plan

If a detailed style is not working, switch to a simpler backup:

- low bun
- side braid
- soft half-up twist
- sleek ponytail with curled ends
- pinned-back waves

These styles can still look elegant, bridal, and polished without taking too much time.

Time-saving tip

Always choose one **main hairstyle** and one **backup hairstyle** before the wedding day.

A backup plan reduces stress and saves the moment.

Emergency Bridal Hair Kit

Keep these items nearby on the wedding day:

- bobby pins
- hair ties
- mini hairspray
- small comb
- tail comb
- anti-frizz serum
- dry shampoo
- decorative pins
- tissues
- small mirror

This small kit can solve most bridal hair emergencies in minutes.

Prepared brides panic less.

Final Troubleshooting Advice

Do not panic if one part of the hairstyle shifts or softens during the day. Wedding hairstyles do not have to stay frozen to stay beautiful. A little softness can still look elegant, romantic, and natural. The goal is not perfect hair every second. The goal is a hairstyle that feels secure, flattering, and true to your wedding look.

Practice before the big day, keep a few essential tools nearby, and remember that calm, simple fixes usually work best.

Confidence is the best finishing touch.

Wedding Morning Game Plan

Your wedding morning can feel exciting, emotional, and a little hectic. That is why having a simple hair plan matter. A beautiful hairstyle is not only about skill. It is also about **timing, preparation, and staying calm.**

This game plan will help you move through the morning step-by-step so your hairstyle looks polished, lasts longer, and feels less stressful to create. The goal is simple: **no panic, no guesswork, no last-minute mistakes.**

A calm plan creates a confident bride.

Start with a Clear Schedule

Do not leave your hair until the last minute. Give yourself more time than you think you need, especially if you are doing your hair yourself or asking a friend or bridesmaid to help.

A good rule is to begin hair styling **at least 2 to 3 hours before you need to get dressed**, depending on the hairstyle. More detailed updos, braids, or curled looks may need extra time. If this is your first time doing the style on a real event day, add at least **30 extra minutes** as a safety buffer.

Build your wedding morning around these stages:

- wake up and freshen up
- light breakfast and water
- skincare and basic prep
- hair preparation
- hairstyle styling
- accessory placement
- final hold check
- getting dressed
- last touch-ups

Buffer means less pressure.

Eat Light and Stay Hydrated

It can be tempting to skip food when you are nervous or busy, but that is a mistake. Have a light meal and drink enough water. Low energy, shakiness, or stress can make styling harder and make the morning feel more overwhelming.

Choose something simple that will not make you feel heavy or uncomfortable. Keep water nearby, but do not overdo it right before dressing if you are already running behind.

A steady body helps create a steady hand.

Calm energy shows in every detail.

Make Sure Your Hair Is Ready

Your hair should already be prepared based on the hairstyle you chose during your trial run. Do not experiment on the wedding morning with a new shampoo, new curling tool, or new styling product.

Before you begin styling, make sure:

- your hair is clean or in the tested condition from your trial
- it is fully dry unless the style calls for damp prep
- your tools are plugged in and working
- your bobby pins, elastics, clips, and spray are nearby
- your accessories are ready and easy to reach

Brush out tangles gently and divide your hair into sections if needed. If your chosen style works better with added texture, apply the same products you used during practice.

Wedding morning is for execution, not experimentation.

Follow the Right Beauty Order

The order of beauty prep matters. If done in the wrong order, you may flatten your hairstyle, disturb your curls, or create unnecessary stress.

A simple order that works for most brides is:

1. basic skincare
2. hair prep
3. hairstyle creation
4. light makeup or full makeup depending on your routine
5. accessory placement
6. final spray and touch-up
7. getting dressed

Some brides prefer makeup before hair, especially if a low bun or pinned style will not be disturbed. Others prefer hair first if curls or structure need time to set. The best choice is the one that matched your trial run.

If you are unsure, test the full order before the wedding day.

The right order protects the final look.

Give Yourself a Styling Buffer

Even if a hairstyle says it takes 15 minutes, that usually means **after practice**. On your wedding day, move more slowly and carefully. If something slips, you want time to fix it without stress.

Add extra time for:

- sectioning the hair
- reheating tools
- adjusting symmetry
- pinning securely
- adding accessories
- final smoothing

Never plan your hair to finish at the exact moment you need to leave. Try to finish at least **30 to 45 minutes early**. That gives you space for photos, touch-ups, deep breaths, and dressing without ruining the style.

Finishing early is a bridal luxury worth planning for.

Add Accessories at the Right Time

Veils, tiaras, combs, flowers, or decorative pins should usually go in **after the main hairstyle is complete**. Do not place them too early, or they may shift while you are still styling.

Before placing accessories:

- check that the hairstyle feels secure
- make sure the front and sides look balanced
- decide exactly where the accessory should sit
- confirm it feels comfortable
- make sure it does not pull the style out of shape

If you are wearing a veil, test whether it should sit above or below the bun or twist. If using flowers, make sure they are pinned firmly but gently. If using a tiara or comb, place it only after the base shape is finished.

Accessories should enhance the style, not fight with it.

Do a Full Mirror Check

Before you say your hairstyle is done, check it from every angle possible. Use a hand mirror or phone camera if needed.

Look for:

- loose pins
- flat crown areas
- uneven sides
- visible elastics
- flyaway
- accessory imbalance
- curls that need reshaping
- loose braid sections

Take one or two quick photos in natural light if possible. Sometimes a style looks fine in the mirror but needs a small fix in photos.

The camera catches what the mirror can miss.

Lock the Style In

Once the hairstyle is complete and checked, set it properly so it lasts. Use a final light mist or stronger hold spray depending on the style. Do not soak the hair. Too much product can make it stiff, sticky, or heavy.

Focus on:

- crown and lift areas
- bun or twist base
- braid hold
- front framing pieces
- accessory support points

If the weather is humid, windy, or hot, use extra care on frizz-prone or loose areas. Keep the finished style untouched as much as possible once it is set.

A strong finish protects all your hard work.

Get Dressed Carefully

Your hairstyle may be perfect, but it can still get ruined while putting on your dress. Be extra careful during this stage.

If possible:

- wear a button-down or zip-front robe while getting ready
- put the dress on gently
- ask someone to help
- protect the hairstyle while changing
- adjust the veil or hair accessories again after dressing if needed

Avoid pulling clothing over your head after the hairstyle is complete unless absolutely necessary.

The final step still matters.

Keep a Small Emergency Kit Nearby

Even the best hairstyle can need a quick touch-up. Keep a small bridal hair kit nearby or ask someone you trust to carry it.

Include:

- bobby pins
- small comb
- mini hairspray
- clear elastics
- tissues
- anti-frizz serum or smoothing cream
- accessory backups
- compact mirror

If you know your hair tends to lose volume, frizz up, or slip out of place, prepare for that in advance.

Small fixes are easier when you are ready for them.

Ask One Person to Be Your Hair Check Helper

Choose one calm and reliable person to do a quick hair check before the ceremony, after dressing, and before photos. This could be your bridesmaid, sister, mother, or close friend.

Tell them what to watch for:

- loose pins
- frizz at the crown
- veil slipping
- flowers falling
- curls dropping
- the back of the hairstyle

This takes pressure off you and helps you stay present in the moment.
A second pair of eyes can save the style.
Stay Calm if Something Shifts
If one section loosens or a curl drops, do not panic. Small issues usually look much bigger to you than they do to anyone else. Pause, breathe, and make a simple fix.

Remember:

- not every strand has to be perfect
- soft movement can still look elegant
- a natural look often photographs beautifully
- confidence makes the hairstyle look even better

Your goal is not robotic perfection. Your goal is to look like the best version of yourself.
Grace always looks beautiful.

Quick Wedding Morning Hair Checklist

Use this checklist before leaving:

Before Styling

[ ] Hair is clean or prepped as tested

[ ] All tools are ready

[ ] Accessories are nearby

[ ] Trial style has been chosen

[ ] Hair products are the same ones used in practice

During Styling

[ ] Hair is sectioned properly

[ ] Style is secure and balanced

[ ] Pins and elastics are hidden

[ ] Front pieces are flattering

[ ] Time buffer is still available

Before Dressing

[ ] Full mirror check done

[ ] Photos checked from front and back

[ ] Accessories placed correctly

[ ] Final spray applied

[ ] Emergency kit packed

Before Leaving

[ ] Veil or headpiece feels secure

[ ] No visible loose sections

[ ] Trusted helper has extra pins

[ ] Style feels comfortable

[ ] Bride feels calm and ready

Prepared brides enjoy the morning more.

Final Thought

A beautiful wedding hairstyle is not only created with pins, curls, and spray. It is created with **good planning, enough time, and a calm start to the day**. Follow your tested routine, give yourself grace, and remember that the most beautiful thing you will wear is your confidence.

A calm morning creates a beautiful memory.

If you want, I can also write the matching **Emergency Bridal Hair Kit** section in the same style so both chapters feel connected.

Emergency Bridal Hair Kit

No matter how carefully you plan your wedding hairstyle, little things can still go wrong. A curl may drop, a pin may loosen, frizz may appear, or your veil may shift out of place. That is why every bride should keep a small **Emergency Bridal Hair Kit** ready on the wedding day. This kit can help you handle quick touch-ups without panic and keep your hair looking neat, elegant, and photo-ready from start to finish.

Your emergency kit does not need to be big. It just needs to include the right items. Place everything in a small pouch or cosmetic bag and give it to a bridesmaid, sister, friend, or anyone who will stay close to you during the event.

What to Keep in Your Emergency Bridal Hair Kit?

Bobby pins

Carry extra bobby pins in colors that match your hair. These are useful for fixing loose twists, buns, braids, or flyaway.

Hair ties or clear elastics

These are helpful if a section comes loose or if a quick re-tie is needed without ruining the style.

Travel-size hair spray

A small hair spray can help control flyaway, add hold, and refresh the shape of your hairstyle after movement, wind, or dancing.

Mini comb or tail comb

A small comb is perfect for smoothing the crown, adjusting parting, or fixing small sections without disturbing the entire look.

Small brush

A compact brush can help soften the front pieces, smooth loose strands, or tidy the back of the hair.

Anti-frizz serum or smoothing cream

A tiny amount can tame frizz, especially in humid weather. Use only a little so the hair does not become greasy.

Hair clips

These are useful while making quick adjustments, especially if you need to lift or hold a section for fixing.

Extra accessories

If you are wearing floral pins, pearls, clips, or a veil comb, carry one or two extras if possible, in case something falls off or gets misplaced.

Mini mirror

A small mirror can help you check the sides or back of your hair if a full mirror is not nearby.

Tissues or blotting paper

These are useful if sweat builds up around the hairline or scalp, especially during warm weather or outdoor weddings.

Cotton swabs

These can help clean up small product smudges near the hairline without ruining makeup or the hairstyle.

Optional Items for Extra Support

Depending on your hairstyle and wedding setting, you may also want to carry:

- dry shampoo for oily roots
- a few U-pins for buns or fuller updos
- a small curling iron or straightener nearby, if time and space allow
- floral wire or extra floral tape for fresh flower hairstyles
- a scarf or soft wrap to protect hair while changing outfits

How to Use the Kit on the Wedding Day

The emergency bridal hair kit should stay close, but it should not stay in your own hands. Give it to someone reliable who understands your hairstyle and knows where the key items are packed. If possible, show that person your final hairstyle before the ceremony and explain what to watch for, such as loose curls, slipping pins, or a shifting veil.

Use the kit only for small fixes. The goal is not to rebuild the hairstyle but to keep it polished and secure throughout the day. A quick spray, one extra pin, or a gentle smoothing touch is often enough.

Pro Tip

Before the wedding day, do one trial run with your emergency kit beside you. This helps you learn which items you actually use and which ones you can skip. It also helps you feel more prepared and confident.

Emergency Bridal Hair Kit Checklist

Use this quick checklist before leaving for the venue:

- extra bobby pins
- extra hair ties or clear elastics
- travel-size hair spray
- mini comb
- small brush
- anti-frizz serum or smoothing cream
- hair clips
- extra accessories
- mini mirror
- tissues or blotting paper
- cotton swabs

A well-prepared bridal hair kit can make a BIG difference. Small fixes done at the right time can keep your hairstyle beautiful, comfortable, and camera-ready all day long.

Prepared brides stay calm. Calm brides look radiant.

Shop Our Recommended products at **MyBrideHairs.com/products**

Practice Makes Perfect

A beautiful wedding hairstyle rarely happens by chance. Even the simplest look becomes smoother, faster, and more polished when you practice it ahead of time. Taking time to rehearse your hairstyle before the wedding day helps you understand what works best for your hair, what tools you need, and how long the style really takes.

Practice is not about making everything perfect on the first try. It is about building confidence. The more familiar you become with a hairstyle, the less stressful the wedding day will feel. You will know which steps are easy, which parts take more time, and what small changes make the biggest difference. That confidence shows in the final result.

Why Practice Matters

Practicing your hairstyle in advance gives you many benefits. It helps you:

- see whether the hairstyle suits your face shape, dress, and wedding theme
- test if the style works well with your hair type and length
- learn how much time you need to complete the style
- discover which products and tools give the best hold
- identify any weak points before the wedding day
- feel calm and prepared instead of rushed and unsure

A hairstyle may look beautiful in a photo, but your practice session will tell you whether it is truly the right fit for YOU. That is the real test.

Practice builds confidence.

When to Start Practicing

Do not wait until the last minute. Start early enough to give yourself room to test, adjust, and improve.

A simple timeline can look like this:

3 to 4 Weeks Before the Wedding

Choose 3 to 5 hairstyles from this book that match your hair type, dress style, and wedding mood. Save photos, gather your tools, and decide which looks you want to test first.

2 Weeks Before the Wedding

Practice your top 2 or 3 favorite styles. Take photos from the front, side, and back. Notice how each hairstyle feels and how long it lasts.

1 Week Before the Wedding

Narrow your choice to 1 main hairstyle and 1 backup option. Practice both again using the exact accessories and products you plan to use on the wedding day.

1 to 2 Days Before the Wedding

Do one final light practice if needed, but avoid overhandling your hair or trying something completely new. By this stage, your decision should already be made.

Start early. Stress less later.

How to Practice the Right Way

When you practice, try to recreate real conditions as much as possible. Use the same tools, the same accessories, and similar hair preparation. If you plan to curl your hair first on the wedding day, do that during practice too. If you plan to wear a veil, clips, pearls, or flowers, test them with the hairstyle.

Practice in front of a mirror with good lighting. Keep a comb, bobby pins, elastics, styling spray, and a hand mirror nearby so you can check the back. Take your time. The first trial is about learning, not rushing.

If possible, wear a top with a neckline similar to your wedding dress. This helps you see how the hairstyle balances your overall look.

What to Look for During Practice

As you test each hairstyle, ask yourself these questions:

- Does this style feel comfortable?
- Does it suit my face and overall bridal look?
- Can I do it myself, or do I need help?
- Does it stay in place for a few hours?
- Will it hold in humidity, wind, or heat?
- Does it still look good from the front, side, and back?
- Does it work well with my veil or accessories?
- Do I feel like myself in this hairstyle?

Your wedding hairstyle should not only look pretty. It should also feel secure, comfortable, and natural for you.

Beauty matters. Comfort matters too.

Take Photos and Notes

Photos are one of the best tools during practice. After each trial, take clear pictures from multiple angles. When you compare them later, you may notice details you missed in the mirror, such as loose sections, flat volume, uneven braids, or visible pins.

It is also helpful to take short notes after every session. Write down:

- hairstyle name
- how long it took
- what products you used
- what worked well
- what needs improvement
- whether you would choose it again

These notes make your final decision much easier.

Try a Full Wear Test

A hairstyle may look great for ten minutes and fail after one hour. That is why at least one of your practice sessions should be a real wear test.

Complete the hairstyle, then leave it in for a few hours. Walk around, move naturally, and see how it holds up. If possible, test it in conditions similar to your wedding environment. For example, if your wedding is outdoors, notice how the style reacts to heat, breeze, or humidity.

A wear test can reveal important things, such as:

- curls dropping too fast
- buns loosening over time
- frizz appearing around the crown
- accessories slipping out
- certain sections feeling too tight or uncomfortable

It is much better to discover these issues early.

Test the hold before the big day.

Practice with Your Accessories

Accessories can completely change how a hairstyle looks and feels. A bun may need extra support once a veil is added. A braided style may look softer with pearls or flowers. A sleek look may become too heavy if the accessory is oversized.

Always test your chosen hairstyle with:

- veil
- tiara or hair vine
- clips or combs
- flowers
- decorative pins

This helps you see how everything works together and whether extra pins or stronger hold are needed.

Know When to Keep It Simple

During practice, you may discover that the most complicated hairstyle is not the best one. That is okay. In fact, many of the most elegant bridal hairstyles are also the simplest.

Choose the hairstyle that gives you the best balance of beauty, comfort, and reliability. A style that looks polished and stays secure is often a better choice than one that is dramatic but difficult to manage.

Do not pick a hairstyle only because it looks impressive in a photo. Pick the one that makes you feel confident and comfortable.

Simple and secure often wins.

Have a Backup Plan

Even after practice, it is wise to keep one backup hairstyle ready. If the weather changes, your hair behaves differently, or you run short on time, a backup option can save the day.

Your backup style should be:

- easier to do
- quicker to finish
- suitable for your hair type
- still beautiful and wedding-worthy

Knowing you have a second option can make you feel much more relaxed.

Final Reminder

Your wedding hairstyle does not need to be perfect on the first try. It only needs preparation, patience, and a little practice. Each practice session brings you closer to a style that feels right for you.

Trust the process. Learn from each trial. Make small adjustments. By the time your wedding day arrives, you will not just be hoping your hairstyle works - you will KNOW it does.

Practice brings confidence. Confidence brings beauty.

Your Final Hairstyle Decision

After exploring different wedding hairstyles, trying a few looks, and learning what works best for your hair, it is time to make your **final hairstyle decision**. This is the style you will trust for one of the most important days of your life, so the goal is not just to choose the prettiest look. The goal is to choose the hairstyle that makes you feel **beautiful, comfortable, confident, and fully yourself**.

A hairstyle may look stunning in a photo, but if it does not suit your hair type, face shape, dress, wedding theme, or comfort level, it may not be the best choice for your special day. Your final hairstyle should bring everything together in a way that feels natural and effortless.

Choose what truly works for YOU.

Start with These 5 Questions

Before making your final decision, ask yourself these simple questions:

1. Does this hairstyle suit my hair type and length?

A style may be gorgeous, but it should also work well with your natural hair. If your hair is short, fine, thick, curly, or layered, choose a hairstyle that complements those features instead of fighting them.

2. Does it match my dress and wedding vibe?

Your hairstyle should feel like part of the full bridal look. A soft braided crown may suit a romantic garden wedding, while a sleek low bun may work beautifully for a classic or modern ceremony.

3. Will I feel comfortable wearing it for hours?

Your wedding hairstyle should not only look good at the start of the day. It should also stay comfortable through the ceremony, photos, greetings, meals, and dancing. If a style feels too tight, heavy, or hard to maintain, it may not be the right choice.

4. Can it hold up in my wedding setting?

Think about the weather, venue, and timing. Outdoor weddings, beach weddings, and humid weather may need stronger hold and simpler structure. Choose a style that will stay secure in your real environment.

5. Do I feel like myself in this hairstyle?

This is one of the most important questions of all. Your wedding look should still feel like **YOU**. The right hairstyle should enhance your beauty, not make you feel like you are pretending to be someone else.

Beauty matters. Comfort matters. CONFIDENCE matters most.

Narrow It Down to Your Top 3

If you still have several favorite hairstyles, narrow them down to your top three choices. Compare them using the points below:

- Which one felt easiest to manage?
- Which one looked best in photos?
- Which one stayed in place the longest?
- Which one matched your dress best?
- Which one made you feel the most confident?

Sometimes the best hairstyle is not the fanciest one. It is the one that feels balanced, polished, and stress-free.

Choose a Main Style and a Backup Style

It is always smart to choose:

- **one final hairstyle**
- **one backup hairstyle**

Your backup style should be simple, reliable, and easy to create if weather, timing, or hair condition changes at the last minute. This helps reduce stress and gives you peace of mind.

For example, if your main choice is a soft curled half-up style, your backup could be a romantic low bun or side-swept twist.

A backup plan is not doubt. It is smart preparation.

Do One Final Trial

Before the wedding day, do one final trial of your chosen style. This is your last chance to confirm that everything feels right.

During this final trial, check:

- how long the style takes to create
- whether it feels secure

- whether it looks good from the front, side, and back
- whether your accessories fit properly
- whether it still looks good after a few hours
- whether it matches your makeup, dress, and overall bridal look

Take photos in natural light if possible. Sometimes a style can look different in pictures than it does in the mirror.

Keep Your Final Choice Simple and Clear

Once you decide, write down your final hairstyle details clearly. This is especially helpful if someone else will help you on the wedding day.

My Final Hairstyle

Style Name: _______________________________________

Why I chose it:

Best features of this style:

Accessories I will use:

Products and tools needed:

Estimated styling time: _______________________________

Backup hairstyle: _________________________________

Helper notes:

This small planning step can save a lot of confusion later.

Trust Your Decision

Once you have chosen your hairstyle, stop second-guessing yourself. You do not need to keep searching for more and more ideas. At some point, too many choices only create stress.

Trust the style that made you feel the most beautiful, the most comfortable, and the most confident.

Your wedding hairstyle does not need to be perfect in a complicated or dramatic way. It just needs to feel right for **your face, your hair, your dress, and your moment.**

On your wedding day, people will remember your smile, your glow, and your happiness far more than one tiny strand of hair. So, choose well, practice once more, and then enjoy the moment fully.

The right hairstyle is the one that lets you feel like your most beautiful self.

Quick Decision Worksheet

You can also add this at the end of the section:

Final Hairstyle Decision Worksheet

My hair type: _______________________________________

My hair length: _______________________________________

My wedding theme/vibe: _______________________________

My dress neckline/style: ______________________________

My top 3 hairstyles:

  1.

____

  1.

____

  1.

____

My final choice: _____________________________________

My backup choice: ____________________________________

Accessories selected: _________________________________

Products to keep ready: _______________________________

Practice date: ____

Final trial completed: Yes / No

I feel most confident in this style because:

Conclusion

Choosing your wedding hairstyle does not have to feel confusing or stressful. With the right preparation, a little practice, and a style that suits your hair type and wedding vibe, you can create a look that feels both beautiful and natural.

In this book, you have discovered step-by-step wedding hairstyles designed to help you save time while still looking polished and elegant. Whether you choose a timeless bun, soft curls, a braided crown, or a romantic half-up style, the goal is not perfection. It is to feel confident, comfortable, and truly like yourself on your special day.

As you prepare for the wedding, remember to practice your chosen style ahead of time, test your accessories, and keep a few backup pins and products ready. Small steps like these can make a big difference and help everything go more smoothly when the day arrives.

Most importantly, choose the hairstyle that makes you feel happy when you look in the mirror. Trends come and go, but the style that feels right for you will always be the best choice.

Thank you for letting this book be part of your wedding journey. I hope it has given you ideas, confidence, and practical help as you plan one of the most meaningful days of your life.

For more hairstyle inspiration, tips, and bridal beauty ideas, explore more resources from Bella Darby at **MyBrideHairs.com**.

Wishing you a day filled with love, laughter, confidence, and unforgettable memories.

Your perfect bridal look starts with confidence, and now you have it.

Appendix

This appendix is designed to help you stay organized, practice with confidence, and choose your final hairstyle with less stress.

Use these pages during your trial runs, your final preparation week, and on your wedding day.

A beautiful hairstyle starts with a clear plan. **Preparation creates confidence.**

Appendix A

Bridal Hair Glossary

Backcombing / Teasing

A method used to add volume by gently combing sections of hair backward toward the scalp.

Bobby Pins

Small pins used to hold sections of hair in place. For stronger hold, insert two pins in a crossed pattern.

Chignon

A classic low bun placed near the nape of the neck for an elegant bridal look.

Crown Area

The upper part of the head where height and volume are often added.

Curling Iron / Wand

A heated styling tool used to create curls or soft waves.

Dry Shampoo

A product that absorbs oil and adds grip, texture, and volume.

Elastic Band

A hair tie used to secure ponytails, buns, or base sections.

Face-Framing Strands

Small pieces of hair left loose around the face for a soft and romantic finish.

Fishtail Braid

A braid made by crossing small sections from side to side to create a woven effect.

Flyaway

Small loose hairs that stick out from the hairstyle.

Half-Up Hairstyle

A style where part of the hair is pinned up and the rest is left down.

Hair Texture Spray

A product that adds grip and body, especially useful for soft or slippery hair.

Hairspray

A finishing product used to help the hairstyle stay in place.

Heat Protectant

A product applied before heat styling to help reduce heat damage.

Low Bun

A bun placed at the lower back of the head for a soft, graceful look.

Mousse

A lightweight product used to create body and lift.

Sectioning

Dividing the hair into parts before styling.

Side Sweep

A look where the hair is directed to one side for a romantic or glamorous effect.

Updo

A hairstyle where most or all of the hair is pinned up.

Veil Comb

The comb attached to a veil that helps secure it into the hairstyle.

Volume

Fullness in the hair, usually created at the roots or crown.

Wave

A soft bend in the hair, less defined than a curl.

The more you understand the basics, the easier styling becomes. **Knowledge builds confidence.**

Appendix B

Bridal Hair Tools Checklist

Use this checklist before your trial sessions and again before the wedding day.

Essential Tools

[ ] Hairbrush

[ ] Fine-tooth comb

[ ] Tail comb for sectioning

[ ] Bobby pins

[ ] U-pins

[ ] Clear elastics

[ ] Sectioning clips

[ ] Curling iron or wand

[ ] Straightener

[ ] Blow dryer

[ ] Mirror

[ ] Handheld mirror for the back view

Styling Products

[ ] Heat protectant

[ ] Hairspray

[ ] Texture spray

[ ] Dry shampoo

[ ] Smoothing serum

[ ] Mousse

[ ] Anti-frizz product

Accessories

[ ] Veil

[ ] Tiara

[ ] Hair comb

[ ] Decorative pins

[ ] Floral accessories

[ ] Pearl pins

[ ] Extra elastics

[ ] Extra bobby pins

Optional Extras

[ ] Shine spray

[ ] Travel-size spray

[ ] Edge brush

[ ] Teasing brush

[ ] Bun maker

Good styling is easier when everything is ready before you begin. **Preparation saves time.**

Shop Our Recommended products at **MyBrideHairs.com/products**

Appendix C

7-Day Bridal Hair Prep Plan

7 Days Before

- Finalize your hairstyle choice
- Do a full trial run
- Take front, side, and back photos
- Check whether the style suits your dress and accessories

5 Days Before

- Test the hairstyle with your chosen accessories
- Check how well it lasts
- Note what worked and what needs improvement

4 Days Before

- Trim split ends only if needed
- Avoid major haircut or color changes

3 Days Before

- Practice the final hairstyle again
- Gather all tools, products, and accessories in one place

2 Days Before

- Wash and condition your hair if needed
- Avoid heavy products unless your hair is very dry

1 Day Before

- Pack your hair kit
- Set aside all accessories
- Avoid trying any new product

Wedding Day

- Begin with dry, detangled hair
- Style calmly and in the right order
- Add accessories after the hairstyle is secure
- Do a final mirror check before leaving

The best bridal hairstyle is not only pretty. It is planned, tested, and trusted. **That is the real secret.**

Appendix D

Wedding Morning Hair Checklist

Before Styling

[ ] Hair is ready as planned

[ ] Hair is fully dry

[ ] Tools are plugged in and ready

[ ] Products are nearby

[ ] Accessories are easy to reach

During Styling

[ ] Hair is sectioned neatly

[ ] Each section is pinned securely

[ ] Crown volume looks balanced

[ ] Front pieces are soft and flattering

[ ] The hairstyle feels comfortable

Before the Final Spray

[ ] Veil placement checked

[ ] Hair accessories placed properly

[ ] Back view checked

[ ] Side view checked

[ ] Flyaway smoothed

Final Check

[ ] Hairstyle feels secure

[ ] The hairstyle suits the dress neckline

[ ] Accessories match the overall look

[ ] Emergency kit is packed

[ ] Backup pins are with a helper or bridesmaid

A calm final check can prevent last-minute stress. **Check once, breathe easier.**

Appendix E

Bridal Hair Emergency Kit

Pack these items in a small pouch and keep it nearby throughout the day.

[ ] Bobby pins

[ ] U-pins

[ ] Clear elastics

[ ] Small comb

[ ] Mini hairspray

[ ] Anti-frizz serum

[ ] Tissues

[ ] Compact mirror

[ ] Extra decorative pins

[ ] Small edge brush

[ ] Safety pins

[ ] Cotton swabs

[ ] Hair tie

Helpful Tip

Give this pouch to your maid of honour, bridesmaid, sister, or another trusted helper.

Smart brides do not rely on luck. They prepare for quick fixes. **That is real confidence.**

Appendix F

Trial Run Tracker

Use this page to compare different hairstyle options.

Style Name:

Trial Date:

Best For:

[ ] Ceremony

[ ] Reception

[ ] Engagement

[ ] Bridal Shower

[ ] Bridesmaid Look

Hair Condition Used for Trial:

[ ] Freshly washed

[ ] Second-day hair

[ ] Curled first

[ ] Straightened first

Time Taken:

Difficulty Level:

[ ] Easy

[ ] Medium

[ ] Hard

What I Liked:

What Did Not Work:

Did It Hold Well?

[ ] Yes

[ ] Somewhat

[ ] No

Best Accessories for This Style:

Would I Choose This for My Wedding?

[ ] Yes

[ ] Maybe

[ ] No

A trial run turns guesswork into clarity. **Practice creates peace of mind.**

Appendix G

Style Comparison Chart

You can expand this chart using all the hairstyles in the book.

Style Name	Hair Length	Hair Type	Skill Level	Time Needed	Veil Friendly	Best For
Simple Chignon	Medium to Long	Straight / Wavy	Easy	10 to 15 min	Yes	Classic bridal look
French Twist	Medium to Long	Straight / Wavy	Medium	About 15 min	Yes	Elegant formal wedding
Braided Crown	Medium to Long	Wavy / Curly	Medium	About 15 min	Optional	Romantic or boho look
Half-Up Half-Down	Medium to Long	Most types	Easy	10 to 12 min	Yes	Soft romantic style
Messy Bun	Medium to Long	Wavy / Curly	Easy	About 10 min	Optional	Rustic or relaxed wedding
Sleek Bun	Medium to Long	Straight	Medium	12 to 15 min	Yes	Modern polished look
Side-Swept Curls	Medium to Long	Wavy / Curly	Medium	About 15 min	Optional	Glam bridal style
Short Hair Twist	Short	Straight / Wavy	Easy	8 to 10 min	Optional	Minimal bridal look

When styles are easier to compare, the final decision becomes easier too. **Clarity saves time.**

Appendix H

Final Hairstyle Decision Page

My Wedding Theme:

My Dress Neckline:

My Hair Type:

My Hair Length:

My Top 3 Hairstyle Choices:

   1.

   1.

   1.

My Final Choice:

My Backup Style:

My Chosen Accessories:

Notes for My Helper or Stylist:

A final decision page turns ideas into a real plan. **Choose with confidence.**

Appendix I

More Bridal Hair Resources

For more bridal hair inspiration, hairstyle ideas, and bridal beauty tips, visit:

MyBrideHairs.com

You can also explore more bridal beauty books and guides by **Bella Darby**.

Download your free bridal hair planning bonus at **MyBrideHairs.com/ bridal-kit** and continue your wedding beauty journey with confidence.

—-***—-

www.ingramcontent.com/pod-product-compliance
Lightning Source LLC
Chambersburg PA
CBHW072009170726
47999CB00014B/1368